THE WORK OF A MAGISTRATE

THE WORK OF A MAGISTRATE

Alan Maddox LL.B

Solicitor and Notary Public

FIFTH EDITION

Shaw & Sons

Published by
Shaw & Sons Limited
Shaway House
21 Bourne Park
Bourne Road
Crayford
Kent DA1 4BZ

© Shaw & Sons Limited 1994

First Published ....January 1964
Second Edition ....July 1969
Third Edition ....April 1975
Fourth Edition ....September 1980
Fifth Edition ....January 1994
Reprinted ....June 1997

ISBN 0 7219 0562 5

A CIP catalogue record for this book is available from the British Library

Printed in Great Britain by
Biddles Short Run Books, King's Lynn

SUMMARY OF CONTENTS

DETAILED TABLE OF CONTENTS

PREFACE

Lay magistrates are chosen from those who have made a success of their own particular callings or are already engaged in public life. They are busy men and women with little time for studying. Furthermore, few of them have ever been in a court before being appointed to the Bench.

Much is now done by means of lectures to prepare newly appointed magistrates for their responsibilities, but a judicial role is never an easy one to play. In spite of the lectures, many magistrates do not understand the rules of evidence and procedure or their purposes; they find it difficult to relate what they are told during lectures to the practical problems of the court-room; and, all too often, the behaviour of professional advocates remains incomprehensible to them.

This book, which is deliberately simple and lacking in detailed references to acts of Parliament and decided cases, is intended to guide magistrates, be they potential, new or experienced, through the many problems that beset them.

But this book is not intended for lay magistrates alone. After all, the Bench (whether lay or professional) cannot play its role in isolation. Only if the Bench, their court clerk and, particularly, the advocates, properly play their particular roles can a Bench do justice – and to do justice is the only proper purpose of any Bench.

It is with this fact in mind that much that concerns the advocate – whether a lawyer or not – has been included in the book. A magistrate cannot properly play his role if he does not understand the purposes of and restrictions on the advocates who appear before him. And, equally, an advocate cannot be effective if he is ignorant of the duties and responsibilities of those before whom he appears.

Thus, this book has been written with the lay and professional advocates who appear in the Magistrates' Court in mind as much as the lay magistrates.

It is recognised, of course, that a large proportion of the

magistracy is female. However, the various statutes and regulations currently use the terms "chairman" and "he".

In order to avoid cumbersome phraseology, this has been followed throughout this book. It is hoped that all readers will appreciate that this is purely as a matter of convenience and implies no discriminatory intention.

My extreme gratitude goes to my previous co-author Brian Fraser Harrison for giving me yet again this opportunity to write this edition and to the court clerks at Wirral Borough Magistrates' Court in Birkenhead for their advice and assistance, even though at the time they were probably unaware of the true purpose and motive behind my "brainpicking". My thanks also to David Hubber, Chairman of the South-Eastern Division of the Inner London Bench, for reading and commenting upon my draft text.

Alan Maddox
Wirral
October 1993

INTRODUCTION

We in England and Wales are fortunate that of the many occupants of our judicial Benches only a few hundred or so are full-time professionals; and that the remainder, called Magistrates or Justices of the Peace generally are ordinary lay people: labourers, housewives, trades union officials, accountants, company directors, and so on.

The preponderance of part-time amateur magistrates over full-time judges is a principal reason why most decisions of our courts, particularly our criminal and matrimonial courts, generally reflect public opinion accurately.

A magistrate in society

To his acquaintances, a magistrate is a magistrate while he is both on and off the Bench; and the magistracy as a whole is judged by the behaviour of each individual magistrate whether in his public, business or social circle. "Fancy him doing that, and him a magistrate too!" is an inevitable criticism that a magistrate must accept; so he must always be honest and dignified (but never mistake pomposity for dignity).

The tasks of a magistrate

A magistrate is required to:

1. Try criminal and civil cases as a judge sitting in a public court.

2. Both in court and elsewhere, undertake various administrative responsibilities, including the control of the sale of liquor, the opening of betting shops, the disposing in a safe place of children in need of protection and, in some circumstances, the destruction of food intended for sale yet unfit for human consumption.

3. Undertake a number of social obligations for individual members of the public, such as the taking of oaths and declarations and witnessing signatures.

4. Grant warrants to police officers for searching premises, the arrest of suspects and extensions of time to retain

suspects in custody pending further enquiries before they are charged and make an appearance in a Magistrates' Court.

A crime and a civil wrong

A crime and a civil wrong are both:

a) the doing of something forbidden by the law; or

b) the failure to do something required by the law.

A crime, however, is an act or omission of such a nature as to require the State (usually as represented by a government or police official) to intervene and have the offender punished. A purpose of a criminal prosecution is the punishment or rehabilitation of a proved offender.

A civil wrong, on the other hand, is an act or omission:

a) that causes a third party an actual or notional suffering that can be measured in money; or

b) in respect of which the law entitles an affected third party to a remedy other than the payment of money.

The purpose of a civil trial is the redress of a proved wrong by compelling restitution or the payment of compensation to the injured party or, in some other manner, the alleviation of the effect of the wrong.

The same act or omission may give rise to both a criminal prosecution and a civil action. A motorist who was involved in an accident in which a pedestrian was injured, for instance, may be both prosecuted on behalf of the State in a criminal court for "reckless driving" and sued by the pedestrian for damages in a civil court. In such an event the criminal proceedings usually, but do not necessarily, precede the civil action. The motorist's acquittal or conviction of the criminal charge has no binding effect on the decision of the judge who tries the civil action.

Superior courts that concern a magistrate

While acting in his public office, a magistrate is required to be guided by and have regard for the pertinent decisions of the judges of the superior courts.

The courts in which a magistrate needs to be interested are:

1. The courts of:

   a) the Queen's Bench;

   b) the Family Division of the High Court,

   which act as appeal courts on questions of law in appeals from the Magistrates' Courts in (a) criminal and (b) family and children cases respectively.

2. The Crown Court to which magistrates (examining magistrates) presiding over a Committal Court commit for trial (send) those who are accused of serious crimes and against whom a *prima facie* case has been made out and where they may send a convicted person for sentence if they feel their own powers are not sufficient.

   A Crown Court is presided over by a judge who sits alone or with magistrates as prescribed by law, although in practice magistrates rarely sit on trials. There are three categories of judges:

   (i) High Court Judges who travel round the six circuits of England and Wales, stopping at the principal centres to preside over the trials by jury of those charged with serious criminal offices.

   (ii) Circuit Judges who may sit with magistrates trying all sorts of criminal matters with or without a jury. Circuit Judges also try civil actions in other courts.

   (iii) Recorders who may sit with magistrates trying criminal matters with or without a jury. Recorders are qualified solicitors or barristers and are generally part-time.

3. The Crown Court as an Appeal Court

   For many matters the Crown Court is an Appeal Court from the Magistrates' Court. An appeal takes the form of a fresh trial.

   During the hearing of an appeal from the Magistrates' Court, the Crown Court Bench acts as both judge and jury, deciding all questions of both law and fact.

The judge and the magistrates who have been invited to attend sit together on the Bench and collectively play the role of a single judge. A judge may sit alone if no other magistrate is available.

Magistrates are most fortunate that they are from time to time required to sit on the Bench at the Crown Court and should take every available opportunity of doing so. Thereby they learn how a court should be conducted; how the various rules of evidence are applied and, in particular, how advocates behave in the presence of a qualified chairman and a shorthand writer who records all that is said.

The functions of a judge and a jury

During a trial, broadly speaking, a judge:

a) rules on all disputes as to the trial's procedure;

b) decides what information is admissible as evidence; and

c) advises the jury as to the pertinent law.

The jury decides all questions of fact and, in particular, the guilt or innocence of the accused.

Magistrates' Courts

The correct and usual title of this court is Magistrates' Court. Such a court may also be referred to as a Petty Sessions, a Petty Sessional Court, a Summary Court, or a Court of Summary Jurisdiction.

Each county is divided into petty sessional divisions to which are allocated a number of the magistrates on the county's Commission of the Peace. Each petty sessional division has at least one court building or shares one with an adjoining division. Generally, the judicial work of a division must be done in its court building.

The frequency with which a Magistrates' Court sits depends on the amount of work required of it: some sit twice monthly, others twice daily.

CHAPTER 1

THE HISTORY OF MAGISTRATES AND HOW THEY ARE NOW APPOINTED

The office of Justice of the Peace was first mentioned in an Act of 1361.

The fourteenth century was one of the most troubled yet socially formative periods of our history. The Black Death struck down the mighty and the unimportant, depopulating large tracts of the country. Soldiers discharged from the French wars returned to find the social structure that they had known slowly disintegrating and hastened that disintegration by robbing and looting. Those feudal lords who survived the plague and could perhaps have maintained order either added to the chaos by quarrelling amongst themselves or abandoned their domestic responsibilities to fight abroad.

Edward III, faced with a country on the verge of anarchy, required a body of men who were loyal to and prepared to take orders directly from the Crown, and by the Act of 1361 had it ordered that ".... in every County of England there shall be assigned for the keeping of the peace one Lord and with him three or four of the most worthy in the County".

From the outset the justices were laden with many and varied duties and, in particular, were required to hunt down, apprehend, and judge those who broke the peace within their particular county.

The Tudor sovereigns, desirous of increasing and strengthening their own authority and that of their governments, found the local Justices of the Peace most useful agents. Each sovereign added more and more to the justices' responsibilities until by the reign of Elizabeth I they included the raising and distribution of Poor Relief, ensuring that roads were kept in proper repair, fixing the prices of various commodities and wages, mustering local troops for the sovereign, enforcing the rules of good husbandry, and dealing with those who had the temerity to wear articles of clothing that were not fitting for their station in life.

A justice's task was therefore more difficult and unpleasant than it is today. He was, and is now, an ordinary, though worthy, member of the community who had to live and contend with his neighbours. Yet he was the government's agent and the sovereign's wrath was visited on him, as a lonely individual, if he failed to persuade his neighbours to comply with the government's often unpopular demands. A justice's neighbours were, however, next door while the government was far away in London and, albeit unwillingly, the justices often found themselves standing between the ordinary man and unpopular and improper government demands and decisions. This independence has been handed on from generation to generation and even today, if not abused, is a protection of our freedoms.

From Tudor days until the Industrial Revolution of the late eighteenth and nineteenth centuries, the local justices continued to deal out justice and administer the country. Gradually the office became the prerogative of one class, the squire in the country and the successful merchant in the towns; men who were arrogantly independent of instruction from their superiors and the murmurings of those below and administered their particular areas with a confidence that made for peace, if not equity.

The Industrial Revolution burst on the country, shattering a social structure that had taken years to build up. It broke ties that held manual workers in small, well-knit and easily controlled communities, and sucked the population into ill-prepared towns. It put wealth into the hands of men who, unlike the squire (and to a lesser degree the merchant), could afford to treat employees as though they were inhuman parts of machines. Money, rather than land and commodities became important. Labour was cheap. Local public administration collapsed.

Those who had been local justices either were not available or refused to act in these new and growing towns, with the result that the office became filled by men who were attracted less by its honour than the financial and other advantages that its holder could gain.

Although the rural justices as a whole continued to be men of integrity, many of their urban brothers, particularly those in London and the other large cities, were openly dishonest. So great and numerous became the scandals and abuses that finally only those honest men who had courage would risk social ostracism by accepting office; fortunately there were some such men.

It was the combining of administrative authority and judicial responsibility in one man that made the opportunities to be dishonest so temptingly possible. Also the prevailing system of local government was generally inefficient, and so in 1881 the bulk of the justices' administrative authority was transferred to county and borough councils, leaving the local justices to concentrate on their judicial role.

The appointment of Justices of the Peace is made by the Lord Chancellor or, in certain areas, the Chancellor of the Duchy of Lancaster, on behalf of the Sovereign. The Chancellor's concern is to appoint sufficient justices to deal with the workload and to ensure, so far as is practicable, that local Benches comprise a representative cross-section of the community. The aim is to achieve a reasonable balance of sexes, ages, political views, ethnic origins, background and occupations – not an easy task.

To assist in this selection process an advisory committee exists in each "commission area" and that committee or, more usually, a sub-committee or panel, will interview candidates for the Bench and make recommendations for appointment to the Chancellor, who is responsible for making the final decision. These committees and their workings used to be shrouded in some secrecy, but this is no longer the case and in most areas the names of the members are made public.

Anyone may apply to become a Justice of the Peace, or may nominate anyone else. An application form may be obtained from the clerk of the advisory committee, whose name and address will be obtainable from any Magistrates' Court in the area. The applicant is asked to submit the names of two referees, who may be, but need not necessarily be, magistrates.

The advisory committee is looking for what is sometimes

termed a "judicial attitude"; this basically means ordinary, sound common sense and an ability to look at issues objectively and to come to reasoned decisions. Justices are not appointed on the basis of professional qualifications. All receive basic training both before they start sitting in court and subsequently, and, of course, experience is the greatest teacher.

Some 29,000 lay magistrates, or Justices of the Peace, currently serve in England and Wales. Although great strides have been made in broadening the membership of Benches, it is still quite difficult to recruit certain types of people, particularly manual workers and younger people building careers. Justices are required to sit a minimum of 26 times a year (a sitting is reckoned to be half a day), except in Inner London where the requirement is now 26 full days for most magistrates. Some employers, such as the civil service and local authorities, have a policy of allowing staff a number of days, perhaps 18 or 20, to fulfil their duties, but often justices have difficulty in this area.

Although unpaid, lay magistrates are entitled to claim travelling expenses and a "subsistence allowance", which is a relatively small sum, to cover refreshments and, if they lose earnings, they may claim a loss of earnings allowance up to a limited amount.

Most magistrates, both lay and stipendiary, and many clerks, belong to the Magistrates' Association, a national body which, among other things, makes representations on behalf of magistrates to government, when new legislation is under consideration. The Association produces "guidelines" on sentencing, to assist justices in their deliberations, and publishes a monthly journal.

There are many who think that, even today, the justices have too much administrative authority and that too many men and women are both local councillors and justices. Be that as it may, most present-day justices are well aware that to be appointed to sit in judgment on one's fellows is not only a great honour, but also a great responsibility. So long as most of our justices approach their task in this knowledge and spirit we shall be well served.

CHAPTER 2

A MAGISTRATE IN COURT

None of a magistrate's duties is more important or onerous than those which he undertakes in public in his own court.

Magistrates are required to solve complex legal problems, differentiate between people of truth and perjurers and ensure that the business of their courts is conducted in an orderly manner. All this they are required to do with little legal knowledge, often without the assistance of competent advocates and unprotected by the rules of precedence and etiquette that do so much to enhance the authority of professional judges.

The magistrate who is conscious of his responsibility and is ambitious to do justice:

a) approaches each case with an open and unprejudiced mind and remains undecided until he has heard all the evidence and speeches;

b) is emotionally unaffected by the behaviour of the accused and witnesses, no matter how cruel, discourteous, anti-social, fawning or obsequious;

c) is courteous to those taking part in the trial and listens to the most long-winded and incomprehensible of explanations and arguments with attention and patience;

d) asks the minimum of questions and causes the minimum of interruptions;

e) tries each case only on the evidence;

f) having listened to and carefully considered the evidence, the advocates' speeches, the court clerk's advice, and the opinions of his fellow magistrates, makes the required decision with fearless independence;

g) above all, is and appears to be fair and impartial.

A magistrate and his prejudices

All of us are affected to some degree by our prejudices. All too often, we are unaware of the existence of those prejudices, yet they are easily discerned by others. A magistrate, in particular, must not be influenced by his prejudices against, for example, motorcyclists, teenagers, or women drivers and, equally, by his sympathy for old people, young children and policemen.

When trying a case a magistrate is not concerned with morality, charity or sympathy: it is the legal and not the moral issue that he must decide.

A magistrate's open mind

Children soon learn the advantage of being the first to tell a tale, and to be the first to "get in a story" is as valuable in a court of law as it is elsewhere. Also, it is easier to appear truthful when making an allegation than when denying one.

An accused or a defendant must wait until those who accuse him have told their story to the magistrates before he is able to start making his denials or give his version of the incident.

A magistrate, must, therefore, guard against forming an opinion until he has heard all the evidence called by, and speeches made on behalf of, both sides.

Rightly or wrongly, the British have faith in the questioning of parties and witnesses in a public court as the best means of unearthing the truth; therefore magistrates must permit an accused's advocate to cross-examine vigorously the prosecution's witnesses, be they frail old people or frightened young children. Equally, the prosecutor should test and probe into the accused's defence by rigorous questioning.

A magistrate cannot always guarantee that his verdict is the correct one. Therefore, he should not hold it against, nor additionally punish, an accused whose unsuccessful defence has entailed the vehement questioning and contradiction of a prosecutor's witness.

Legal knowledge

Never is the phrase "A little learning is a dangerous thing" so aptly used as in the case of a lay magistrate.

Our laws are based on the customs of the land (or, to use a more formal phrase, the "Common Law") and Acts of Parliament as interpreted by the professional judges. No sooner does Parliament pass an Act than its meaning is questioned and requires interpretation by the courts. Once a judge of a higher court has interpreted a Statute or given his opinion as to what is the law, brother judges of the same rank must heed his interpretation or opinion and his inferiors are bound by it.

Thus, for practical purposes, the law alters daily and no layman can hope to remain up to date in his legal knowledge; indeed, the law is so complex now that professional lawyers are tending to specialise in only one or two branches of it.

Although lay magistrates are not required to be learned in the law, there is a dangerous tendency on the part of many senior magistrates to assume that they "know" the law. Lay magistrates must realise that a judgment based on imperfect or out-dated information will invariably be wrong; they should, therefore, start every trial without any preconceived notions as to what is the law.

Magistrates will, of course, wish at all times to uphold the dignity of their office but neither they nor their office lose any dignity by admitting in the public court their ignorance of some legal matter. If a magistrate accepts and acts on a legal argument or what he is told by an advocate or his court clerk, without fully understanding the argument and its purpose, he is not acting judicially. If he lacks understanding a magistrate should say so, and should halt the trial until he does understand what he is being told.

Legal quotations

The law involved in most trials is simple, and so the magistrates may concentrate on the various stories as to what occurred in an attempt to learn the truth.

Occasionally, however, the legal issues are complex. Whether, for instance, a building is a "factory" is an issue that may well be taken from the Magistrates' Court to the High Court and thence to the House of Lords.

A magistrate cannot, therefore, be blamed if he approaches a legal problem with some trepidation. He must do his best to interpret the Act or regulation and cases involved. He should make his mind up without being fearful of the disagreement of an appeal court. So long as a magistrate has made a reasonable and independent decision there is no stigma attached to his decision being altered by a higher court.

Prosecuting and defending advocates are under an obligation to tell the Bench of *all* the law involved in a case, whether that law is favourable or adverse to their cause. Of course, once an advocate has told the magistrates of the law (be it an Act of Parliament, regulation or reported case), he may attempt to interpret it in a manner which is favourable to his client.

Usually, advocates do not need to dispute the existence or wording of a Statute or case, only its interpretation. Magistrates may, therefore, usually rely on a quotation from one of the many excellent encyclopaedias or manuals that are available. If, however, such a quotation is seriously disputed by either side, a magistrate would be wise to insist on being shown a copy of the actual Act, regulation or case and ask for the assistance of the court clerk, who will readily advise him as to the law.

The decision is, however, the magistrate's, and he must bear in mind the submissions of the two advocates as well as the clerk's advice when making it.

Magistrates and their court

Magistrates can concentrate on the evidence and arguments and reach a reasonable decision only if the trial proceeds in an orderly manner. The responsibility for ensuring that a trial proceeds in this way is that of the chairman of the Bench and his fellow magistrates should help in this task by playing an almost passive role while in court. If by any chance a magistrate wishes to ask a question (something that should rarely happen), the question should normally be put through the chairman. If the Bench wishes to make a pronouncement, it should be made by the chairman.

Chapter 3

SUMMARY TRIAL PRELIMINARIES

A magistrate will try far more criminal than other types of cases and as the basis of all trials in the magistrates' courts is similar to that of a criminal one, the procedure and essentials of a criminal trial are set out at some length.

Criminal proceedings are started by the physical arrest of an accused or, occasionally, the laying before a magistrate of a document called an Information, in which is set out the accused's name and the alleged offence. If, having heard evidence in support of the information, a Magistrate agrees that the accused should be proceeded against the Magistrate issues either:

a) a warrant authorising the accused's arrest (in which case the information must be in writing and substantiated on oath); or

b) a summons ordering the accused to attend court and answer the specified charge on the day of the trial.

A warrant for the arrest of any person who has attained the age of eighteen shall not be issued unless:

a) the offence to which the warrant relates is an indictable one or is punishable with imprisonment; or

b) the address of the defendant is not sufficiently established for a summons to be served on him.

Should the accused be arrested and not released on bail by the police, he should be brought before a Magistrates' Court as soon as practicable.

When he is brought before the court, an accused may be remanded in custody or on bail.

A remand in custody before an accused has been convicted may not be for a period longer than eight clear days (*e.g.* from a Monday to the Wednesday of the following week).

A remand on bail must also be for a maximum period of eight clear days unless *both* the prosecutor and the accused consent to a longer period.

Bail

Whenever an accused person appears before the magistrates he is entitled to bail regardless of whether or not an application for bail is made. Bail may only be refused under certain prescribed conditions.

To grant an accused bail means that he is allowed his freedom and in return he acknowledges that he is under an obligation to attend on the date and at the time and place appointed. Often an accused's acknowledgement alone is not thought by the magistrates to be sufficient; in that event, before the accused is released from custody, the magistrates may impose conditions on the grant of bail.

When granted bail the accused must agree that he will attend as required and abide by any conditions imposed by the magistrates. If an accused fails to surrender to his bail without reasonable excuse, he commits a further offence. This further offence is arrestable, either with or without a warrant issued by the court and carries its own penalties. This new offence is known as absconding.

Obviously, if the accused refuses to be bound by (or is unable to satisfy) the conditions of his bail, then he remains in custody.

The responsibility for granting or refusing bail and the terms on which bail is granted, is the magistrates' alone. Each application, even when two or more accused are charged together, must be considered on its own merits and there are five matters that must always be borne in mind:

a) bail must never be refused in order to punish an accused: no one may be judicially punished until after he has pleaded guilty or been convicted;

b) unless an accused has made an admission of guilt, the truth of which he does not deny, he is innocent until he is found guilty at his trial;

c) liberty, both our own and that of others, is precious, yet is easily lost if our courts fail to safeguard it for us;

d) it is difficult for an accused to prepare his defence when he is in a prison or remand centre, particularly when he is kept many miles from his solicitor's office;

e) bail must never be refused in order to ensure that an accused is readily available to be interviewed by the police.

A remand to police custody

Magistrates have the power to remand an accused into police custody (in which case he remains in a police station) rather than having him sent to a prison or remand centre.

Normally, such a step is taken only if the trial or committal proceedings of the accused is to take place within the next three days or if the accused's lawyer wishes to interview his client and the nearest prison or remand centre is far away. Obviously, an accused will be remanded into police custody only if the police have the necessary facilities available. Magistrates should not remand an accused into police custody if the accused advances sensible objections to being readily available to visits from and questioning by the police.

The remand into police custody may not be for longer than one period of three clear days and any subsequent remand must be to a prison or remand centre.

Procedure on an application for bail

An accused is entitled to have his bail situation considered every time he appears in court. Whenever an accused asks for bail the magistrates must consider the request with care, even if similar applications by the accused at his earlier appearances in court have been refused, as circumstances may have changed (one of which may well be the increasing delay on the part of the prosecution in readying themselves for the trial).

Whenever an accused wishes to be released on bail:

a) the prosecutor, if he wishes to, says why he thinks the magistrates should not grant bail (he must state categorically what his reasons are);

b) the accused or his advocate may argue why, despite the prosecutor's objection, the accused should be released from custody.

A prosecutor's objections to bail

A prosecutor who objects to an accused being released on bail must tell the magistrates why he objects. Below and on the next page are set out the grounds on any one or more of which the magistrates may refuse bail, and a prosecutor must be able to refer to at least one of those grounds if his objection is to be of value.

Persons under eighteen

Applications of those accused who have not attained eighteen years of age are dealt with in Chapter 7, "Youth Courts".

Everything written on the subject of bail in this chapter refers to those accused who have attained the age of eighteen years.

The two groups of offences

As a result of the Bail Act 1976 a distinction is made as to whether the offence is punishable with imprisonment or not. The exceptions to the right to bail (or the grounds for refusal of bail) differ between the two groups.

Bail. First group – where offence is punishable with imprisonment

When an accused who has attained eighteen years of age is before the magistrates charged with an imprisonable offence and a remand is necessary, the magistrates need not grant bail if they are satisfied that there are substantial grounds for believing that the accused, if released on bail, would:

(i)   fail to surrender to custody;

(ii) commit further offences whilst on bail;

(iii) obstruct the course of justice, e.g. by interfering with a witness.

Magistrates should have regard to certain considerations in taking such a decision:

a) the nature and seriousness of the offence or breach of the requirements of a Probation Order or Community Service Order;

b) the accused's character, antecedents, associations and community ties;

c) the accused's record regarding past grants of bail;

d) the strength of the evidence against the accused (except when a remand for enquiries or a report is to be made);

e) any other considerations which appear to be relevant.

Bail. Second group – where offence is *not* punishable with imprisonment

When an accused who has attained eighteen years of age is before the magistrates on a charge in this group and a remand is necessary, the magistrates must grant bail to the accused except where they believe that an accused who has previously been granted bail and failed to surrender to custody will again fail to surrender to custody.

Unless the accused has previously failed to surrender to custody, the magistrates must grant him bail.

Three further exceptions to bail

There exist three exceptions to bail (or grounds for refusal) which apply to accused from either of the two groups:

(i) if the magistrates are satisfied that the accused needs to be kept in custody for his own protection;

(ii) if the accused is already in custody following sentence;

(iii) if the accused has been released on bail and then arrested for absconding.

The accused who may fail to surrender

Normally, an accused will attend his trial; the number who do not is surprisingly small. When the accused has a home, is living with his family and, particularly, has a business or salaried position, it is unlikely that he will not answer or surrender to his bail.

A lack of a home and a settled job, the likelihood of the accused's going abroad, together with the possible severity of the punishment are examples of the factors that the magistrates should take into consideration when deciding whether to grant or refuse bail.

The accused who commits more offences

There is sometimes the danger that the accused will commit additional offences while he is free on bail and, if the prosecutor thinks that the accused is likely to misbehave, he should object to bail being granted.

When a prosecutor objects to bail on this ground, the magistrates should ask to be told of the accused's earlier convictions.

The mere fact that an accused has already been convicted many times is not alone a good reason for the magistrates to refuse bail; the magistrates must consider both the types of the earlier offences and the charge on which the accused is now before the court. If a man has been convicted twice for indecency and is now before the court for alleged dishonesty, the pattern of misbehaviour has been broken and there cannot be a presumption that the accused will commit a second offence of dishonesty while on bail. Should the accused hitherto have had a good character, he cannot be presumed likely to misbehave while on bail.

An accused's interfering with witnesses or obstructing the course of justice

A third ground for refusing bail is the most troublesome to magistrates: that the accused may persuade or frighten witnesses on whom the prosecutor will rely into lying or refusing to testify or otherwise interfere with the prosecutor's evidence. Fortunately, the number of accused who are likely to consider intimidating the prosecutor's witnesses is small. This is a ground on which the magistrates should be reluctant to refuse bail, doing so only after they are convinced there is a very real danger of the accused misbehaving.

It is important to understand that a witness is not a member of a team: he is not the property of either the prosecutor or the accused, or (in civil cases) the complainant or defendant.

Theoretically and ideally a witness tells all, and only, the truth, no matter who calls him to the witness box. A witness may be interviewed by or on behalf of the prosecutor or the accused. By means of a witness summons, a witness may be compelled to attend court and tell what he knows, but a witness has the right to refuse to discuss the events in question with either party beforehand. Not only may a witness be questioned by either the accused or the prosecutor about the events giving rise to the charge, but he may also be questioned about what was said during his interview with the opposition.

The prosecutor and the accused may see and rigorously question any witness, whether or not that witness has already been interviewed by the other side. But neither side may, by any means, attempt to corrupt a witness.

Thus, bail should not be refused merely because the prosecutor fears one of the witnesses whom he intends to call may be interviewed by the accused. Magistrates must be convinced that the accused intends to intimidate a witness before refusing bail.

Occasionally, a prosecutor says that he objects to bail because a number of enquiries are yet to be made. This is not, in itself, a proper reason for bail to be refused and the magistrates must ask on what specific ground the objection is made; probably it is that the accused is likely to interfere with evidence or witnesses. The magistrates must then allow the accused bail unless they are convinced there is a real risk.

Obviously, it is better that the accused's solicitor, not the accused, interviews witnesses; this is one of the many reasons magistrates should grant legal aid to those who qualify for it as soon as possible.

Committals to a higher court for sentence
Where the magistrates, after an accused has pleaded guilty or been convicted by them, have the power to commit the accused to a Crown Court for him to be sentenced and they exercise that power, they ought to commit the accused *in custody* unless they have a good reason to do otherwise.

The reason for this is fairly obvious; the magistrates will

commit an accused to the higher court only when they consider their own powers of punishment are inadequate and, to allow an accused who knows he is likely to be imprisoned his liberty, is to tempt him to abscond or to live the life of Riley during his few remaining days of freedom.

Remand by the magistrates after a trial

There are occasions when, after an accused has pleaded guilty or been convicted by them, the magistrates wish to learn more about the accused before passing sentence on him. In this event, the magistrates must consider whether or not to permit the accused his freedom on bail while enquiries are made.

Duration of pre-trial remands

An accused whose trial has not been completed may be remanded for:

a) any reasonable period so long as he is released on bail; but

b) for a maximum period of eight clear days if he is kept in custody.

This means that if the date of the accused's trial or committal is not fixed or is some weeks ahead and the accused is not allowed bail, he must be brought before the Magistrates' Court at least every eight days if he is remanded in custody.

This is a valuable right and should be treated as such, and not as a mere formality. At least once every eight days an accused who is being kept in custody makes a public appearance before the magistrates unless he has consented not be produced until a later date. On such appearances he is entitled to make requests (for instance, for bail or legal aid) or to make complaint of the manner in which he is being dealt with or treated, perhaps by those in charge of the prosecution, if they have access to him, or even those responsible for his defence. The accused may also be entitled to complain if there is an inordinate delay in his trial.

A magistrate should recognise how cut off and helpless a person in custody is and, if that person is innocent, how he may suffer emotionally.

Duration of post-trial remands

When an accused has pleaded guilty or been convicted and the magistrates wish to remand him in order that more information, medical or otherwise, about him can be obtained, or if they wish the Probation Service to interview him to prepare Pre-Sentence Reports, they may remand him for:

a) a maximum period of four weeks if he is released on bail; or

b) a maximum period of three weeks if he is kept in custody.

Unconditional bail

Magistrates may grant bail to an accused unconditionally, *i.e.* without attaching any conditions at all to bail. Should the accused fail to surrender to his bail without reasonable excuse, he will have committed a further offence and will be charged with this in addition to the one for which bail was originally granted.

Conditional bail

Magistrates may grant bail to an accused subject to certain conditions.

They may require the accused to provide a surety, that is to say, a person who will be bound in a sum of money to ensure the attendance of the accused at court on the appointed day at the appointed hour. Such a surety will enter into a recognizance with the court in a certain sum of money which will have been fixed by the magistrates and the surety will forfeit all or part of that sum should he or she fail in his obligations to the court.

Sometimes, particularly when the remand would be for a long period if the accused were granted bail, magistrates think that an accused should not lose all contact with those in authority during the interim period. The magistrates may include special conditions on the grant of bail if those conditions appear likely to result in the accused's appearance at the time and place required or to be necessary in the interests of justice or for the prevention of crime.

The accused may not, however, be required to find a surety in respect of a special condition.

Generally speaking, magistrates may impose such conditions as appear to be necessary to secure that:

   a) the accused surrenders to custody;

   b) the accused does not commit an offence while on bail;

   c) the accused does not interfere with witnesses or otherwise obstruct the course of justice in relation to himself or any other person;

   d) the accused makes himself available for the purpose of enabling enquiries or reports to be made to assist the court in dealing with him.

Examples of such conditions are that the accused:

   (i)   should not, either by himself, his servant or agent, approach or communicate with the complainant or other specified person, *e.g.* the main prosecution witness or witnesses;

   (ii) should remain indoors between certain hours (usually the hours of darkness), *i.e.* a curfew;

   (iii) should reside at a fixed and stated address;

   (iv) should report to his nearest police station at fixed times;

   (v) should travel in no vehicle other than a public service vehicle;

   (vi) should not go within one mile of the City Centre;

   (vii) should surrender his passport;

   (viii) should not visit licensed premises.

There is no limit to the variety of conditions which may be attached to the grant of bail, but conditions must be reasonable.

Notices to be given on refusal to grant bail

When magistrates refuse to remand or commit on bail an accused who is at least eighteen years of age and is not represented by a barrister or solicitor, they must tell the accused of his right to apply to a High Court or Crown Court Judge for bail.

Restrictions on magistrates sitting after dealing with bail

Once a magistrate, in order to decide whether or not to grant an accused bail, is told that the accused has one or more previous convictions, the magistrate may not later take part in summary trial in the same proceedings as to whether or not the accused is innocent or guilty. This rule applies even when a magistrate and a colleague are sitting as examining magistrates and decide to cease proceeding as examining magistrates and to try the case summarily.

There is nothing to prevent a magistrate who has learned of an accused's previous convictions sitting as an examining magistrate at a committal, since he is not required to decide guilt or innocence, but merely whether or not the prosecutor has made out a *prima facie* case against the accused. Similarly, there is nothing to prevent a magistrate with knowledge of an accused's previous convictions from dealing with subsequent applications for bail and sentencing an accused who has pleaded guilty at his summary trial.

Obviously, these restrictions are put on a magistrate in order to prevent his decision being influenced by knowing that the accused has been previously convicted. It is not easy to believe a man's vehement denial of guilt when you know that he has a string of convictions, especially if the convictions are for the same offence as that with which he is currently charged. Peculiarly, however, a magistrate is forbidden to try an accused summarily only if he has learned of the accused's previous convictions in the *same* proceedings, *i.e.* during those remands that preceded the current summary trial. There are no *legal* objections to a magistrate's summarily trying an accused he has summarily tried before, no matter how often or on what charges.

Even if there is no legal objection, if a magistrate has the slightest doubt as to whether he can try an accused impartially since he knows that the accused has previous convictions, he should refuse to sit in judgment on him.

Written copies of decisions

Where conditional or unconditional bail is granted or refused, an accused is entitled to a copy of the decision and, in the case of a conditional grant, refusal or variation of any previous condition, the magistrates must give their reasons. This is to enable the accused to consider making an application in the matter to another court.

Remands and adjournments

It is not unusual for either a prosecutor or an accused to ask a Bench to postpone an accused's trial. When an accused has been arrested, only rarely are the prosecutor and accused ready for a trial on the accused's first appearance in court. Occasionally, even a summoned accused has not had time to prepare his defence. Not infrequently a witness whom one or other side needs to call is ill, or an advocate is otherwise engaged. In such circumstances, the magistrates are asked to adjourn the trial.

Generally, applications made on behalf of an accused should be agreed to: he must never be in a position to say with truth that he was not given sufficient time to prepare his defence.

When the accused is not to be remanded in custody, an application for the adjournment of a trial by the prosecutor may be granted fairly readily. If an accused objects to the adjournment *and* is to be kept in custody during it, the magistrates should not agree to the postponement unless the prosecutor's need for it is, without question, a valid one.

One of the most common reasons for an application for an adjournment is for the defence to apply to the Crown Prosecution Service for an "advance disclosure".

Under certain circumstances the prosecution are obliged to supply the defence with details of evidence in their possession in advance of a plea being entered. This normally takes the form of supplying details of prosecution witnesses' statements and copies of any tape recorded interviews that took place in police stations.

The magistrates' responsibility

The decision to grant or refuse the postponement of a trial is the magistrates' and in theory none should anticipate it. On the other hand, expense and time is saved if witnesses are prevented from attending court unnecessarily. It is helpful if the prosecutor and accused's advocate are permitted to agree between themselves to postponements and discuss their agreement with the justices' clerk as soon as possible. Magistrates can soon control any abuse of their leniency in this respect.

When an application to postpone a trial is made, magistrates must never take into consideration their own or the court's convenience. The fact that the magistrates will be left with little or no judicial work that day is no reason to refuse a postponement.

Procedure when an arrested man is remanded

As stated earlier, an arrested man *who has been kept in custody* must be brought before a Bench of magistrates as soon as reasonably practicable following his arrest or on the day following an intervening Sunday, Good Friday or Christmas Day.

On the accused's first appearance in court, the magistrates must be satisfied that the alleged offence has been committed and that the accused is likely to be the malefactor: the rule against hearsay evidence is not strictly enforced at this moment.

Some courts, but not all, insist on evidence of arrest being given. There is, however, no legal requirement that it *must* be given.

The accused has the right on every appearance in court to:

    a) question the witness giving evidence of the arrest;

    b) object to an adjournment;

    c) ask for bail;

    d) ask for legal aid.

Although magistrates may, for the sake of convenience, allow the prosecutor and the accused's advocate to agree that a particular trial will be adjourned, an accused who has been bailed to attend court must attend on the due date to have his bail renewed or (as is always possible, although unlikely) to be remanded in custody.

Procedure on the adjournment of a summons

The adjournment of the hearing of a summons (other than one in respect of an indictable offence) does not normally require the attendance of the defendant or the same formalities as the remand of an arrested accused.

In the case of a summons in respect of an indictable offence, an accused adult must be remanded, which normally involves the question of bail. In such cases, an accused adult must attend in person.

Should the magistrates permit the prosecutor and the accused to agree between themselves that the trial be postponed, the magistrates may well save time by dispensing with the attendance at court of an accused summoned for a summary offence and his advocate. The prosecutor will mention the postponement to the magistrates. No doubt, either the prosecutor or the accused's advocate will already have discussed the new date with the court clerk.

Delays in trials

The work Magistrates' Courts are required to do is increasing, and there is often a long delay between the alleged crime and the accused's trial.

An accused who is arrested is fortunate in that he soon learns, at least in general terms, of the allegations that he will have to meet and can make his preparations.

A man who is brought before the court by means of a summons is often at a disadvantage in this respect: as much as three (sometimes even more) months may elapse after the incident before the summons is served, yet the period between receipt of the summons and the trial may be much shorter. This obviously is unfair to the accused, who has little chance of discovering witnesses and otherwise preparing his defence. Magistrates and their clerks should encourage those responsible for prosecutions to have informations laid and summonses served as soon as possible after the alleged offence, even if there is then a long delay before the trial. Indeed, some prosecuting authorities are conscious that it is unfair on accused persons when there is a long delay between the commission of the alleged offence and the issue of the process. Such authorities try to ensure that the decision to prosecute is made and the appropriate process issued as soon as possible after the alleged offence is reported.

Chapter 4

SUMMARY TRIAL PROCEDURE

Starting the trial

1. The court clerk asks the accused to identify himself.

2. Most court clerks ask an unrepresented accused whether he is ready for the trial to proceed and, if the charge is a serious one, whether he wishes to have time to instruct a solicitor.

3. The court clerk reads out the charge or summons and explains it to the accused in every-day language.

4. The court clerk asks the accused or his solicitor whether he has applied to the Crown Prosecution Service for advance disclosure, *i.e.* detailed information about evidence in the possession of the prosecution.

5. The court clerk's next step depends on the class of offence before the magistrates. There are three classes of offence:

   a) offences triable only on indictment, *i.e.* at a Crown Court.

   b) offences triable only summarily, *i.e.* at a Magistrates' Court.

   c) offences triable either way, *i.e.* at a Crown Court or a Magistrates' Court.

The court clerk will advise magistrates which offences fall into which class although, with experience, magistrates usually acquire a basic knowledge of offences and classes.

In the case of offences triable on indictment, magistrates will usually remand the accused to a committal court to be held at a future date.

In the case of offences triable either way the magistrates, as a preliminary step, must consider whether the offence appears more suitable for summary trial or for trial on indictment.

Before the magistrates consider this, the charge should be

read to the accused, whereupon the magistrates must afford first the prosecutor and then the accused an opportunity of making representations as to which mode of trial would be more suitable.

The factors which the magistrates must take into account when reaching their decision are:

(i) the nature of the case;

(ii) whether the circumstances make the offence a serious one;

(iii) whether the punishment a magistrates' court would have power to inflict would be adequate;

(iv) any other circumstances which make it more suitable for the offence to be tried in one way than the other.

The preference of the prosecutor is never binding and magistrates should not place greater weight on his representation than that of the accused.

The accused, on the other hand, has an unfettered right to require trial on indictment, notwithstanding representations made by the prosecutor to the contrary, but his right to require summary trial is equal to that of the prosecutor.

If the magistrates decide that the case is more suitable for trial on indictment, the accused is told that the magistrates will not hear it and, if all parties are ready, committal proceedings take place but in nearly all cases the accused is remanded to a future committal date.

If the magistrates decide that the case is more suitable for trial summarily then:

1. The court clerk explains to the accused in ordinary language that it appears to the court more suitable for him to be tried summarily for the offence and he can either consent to be so tried or, if he wishes, be tried by a jury. Should the accused elect to be tried by a judge and jury, the magistrates may, there and then, start the committal proceedings or, as is more usual, remand the accused to a committal court to be held on a future date.

2. The court clerk also tells the accused that if he is tried summarily and either pleads guilty or is convicted by the magistrates, then, if on having obtained more detailed information about the accused and the case, the magistrates are of the opinion that greater punishment should be inflicted than they have power to inflict, the magistrates may commit him to the Crown Court for sentence.

Magistrates' possible bias

Assuming that the case is to be tried summarily, it is at this moment that the accused should make his objection to being tried by a particular magistrate and, unless the objection is frivolous, the magistrate should retire from the Bench.

Even if no objection is taken to his trying a case, a magistrate should retire if:

a) he knows well either party or a witness;

b) he is in the remotest way interested in or affected by the result of the trial;

c) he has been approached about the case or has discussed the case or the parties;

d) he has already formed an opinion about the case.

At the outset of a trial, a magistrate does not always know the identity of the witnesses who will be called during it and therefore may not know he is acquainted with one of them until they enter the witness box.

When a magistrate realises he is so well acquainted with a witness that his relationship with that witness may conflict with his judicial duty, he must immediately withdraw from the Bench. He must also withdraw when he finds he is directly or indirectly concerned in the subject of the proceedings (for instance, if he is a councillor and the charge involves his council's property).

When a magistrate finds it necessary to withdraw from the proceedings, he should leave the Bench altogether and not merely push his chair back.

When the magistrate has only one other magistrate sitting

with him, the trial must be halted and later recommenced before another Bench. This is unfortunate, but necessary.

Occasionally, the parties or their advocates may announce that they have no objection to a magistrate who should otherwise retire continuing to adjudicate. When this happens, a magistrate may perhaps continue to adjudicate if he is absolutely certain that his decision will be influenced only by what is properly related to him during the trial.

Certainly, no party or advocate should be asked if he agrees to a magistrate who would otherwise have to leave the Bench continuing to adjudicate. An advocate (particularly one appearing in a small rural court), may feel that he would prejudice his future appearance before a magistrate to whom he had, in effect, said, "I do not trust you to be unbiased" and may agree, from necessity not choice, to the magistrate's continuing to sit.

If ever a magistrate has the slightest doubt as to whether he should continue to adjudicate, he should resolve that doubt by leaving the Bench.

Charges dismissed or withdrawn

Occasionally, for one reason or another, the prosecutor asks the permission of the Bench to withdraw a charge. When this happens, the accused should be told of the difference between a charge being:

a) dismissed for want of prosecution, and

b) withdrawn.

When a charge is dismissed for want of prosecution, after the accused has pleaded "Not Guilty", the accused has been in peril on that charge, and may not be brought before a court to answer that same charge again. If, however, a charge is merely withdrawn, the accused has never been in peril and may be brought back to court on that particular charge sometime in the future, although in practice it is unlikely.

The plea

Next, the plea is taken by the court clerk asking the accused whether he pleads:

a) Guilty; or

b) Not Guilty.

When an accused is before the court on more than one charge, a separate and distinct plea must be taken to each charge.

Should there be the slightest doubt as to the accused's understanding of the charge or acknowledgement of his guilt, a plea of "Not Guilty" must be entered.

Procedure after a plea of "Guilty"

After a plea of "Guilty":

a) the prosecutor, briefly and without undue emphasis, relates the circumstances of the offence and such law as is pertinent to it (magistrates should discourage prosecutors from using colourful and dramatic language);

b) the court clerk asks the prosecutor:

   (i)   whether anything is known about the offender and, in particular, of any previous convictions;

   (ii) whether he is requesting that the offender should contribute towards the costs of the prosecution;

c) if the offence is one for which the offender's driving licence may be endorsed, the court clerk asks the offender to produce his driving licence;

d) if Pre-Sentence Reports have been ordered, the Bench read the reports, or if Pre-Sentence Reports are thought necessary but have not been made, the accused may be remanded in custody or on bail so that the enquiries may be made;

e) the offender or his advocate makes a speech of excuse or explanation (called a speech in mitigation);

f) the magistrates sentence the offender.

The fact that an offender pleads guilty does not necessarily mean that he accepts as true all that the prosecutor says of the facts of the offence. For instance, a motorist who has driven at 36 m.p.h. and pleads guilty to exceeding a 30 m.p.h. speed limit could and should dispute the prosecutor's allegation that his speed was 50 m.p.h.

There is no laid down procedure to be followed when there is a dispute such as this; the Bench must give what it thinks is the appropriate weight to each version and try to decide on the appropriate penalty.

Procedure after a plea of "Not Guilty"

The steps of a summary trial are:

a) unless the advocates agree to the contrary, all witnesses are ordered to leave the court;

b) if there be an interpreter, he is sworn;

c) the prosecutor *may* make an opening speech;

d) the prosecutor calls his witnesses, each of whom is:

   (i) examined-in-chief by the prosecutor;

   (ii) cross-examined by the accused or his advocate;

   (iii) re-examined by the prosecutor;

e) the prosecutor announces that he has closed his case;

f) the accused or his advocate may submit that the accused has no case to answer;

g) the prosecutor may reply to any point of law (but not to anything about the facts) raised by the accused or his advocate during the latter's submission of "No Case to Answer";

h) the accused or his advocate may answer the prosecutor's reply to the submission of "No Case to Answer";

i) the magistrates rule on the submission of "No Case to Answer";

j) if no submission of "No Case to Answer" is made or the magistrates rule that there is a case to answer, the accused or his advocate *may* make an opening speech;

k) the accused testifies and is followed into the witness box by his witnesses, and the accused and his witnesses are:

  (i) examined-in-chief;

  (ii) cross-examined;

  (iii) re-examined;

l) the prosecutor may, in certain circumstances, call rebutting evidence;

m) the final speech is or speeches are made;

n) the magistrates decide on their verdict;

o) the chairman announces the verdict;

p) if the accused has been acquitted he may apply for his costs and, when that application has been dealt with, the accused is released; but

q) if the accused has been convicted, the magistrates receive any reports on the accused that have been prepared and are told by the police of any previous convictions of the accused. Should no Pre-Sentence Reports have been obtained, the magistrates may remand the accused on bail or in custody for the reports to be obtained (the same Bench need not necessarily attend on the new date);

r) the accused or his advocate may address the Bench about the accused's punishment;

s) after the magistrates have considered and agreed on the sentence, the chairman announces it.

Witnesses out of court

When either advocate or party so requests or the magistrates think it proper, all witnesses of both sides, including police officers, are caused to leave the court before the trial starts. Of course, the accused may not be ordered to leave the court and may insist on being present throughout his trial and it is usual to halt his trial if, for any reason, he has to be absent.

An accused must be present throughout his committal, but some summary trials may take place in the absence of the accused. Magistrates presiding over a summary trial would be wise to be guided by their court clerk as to whether or not they may proceed in the accused's absence.

The interpreter

Should one be necessary, an interpreter is sworn and, as necessary, interprets what is said during the trial.

The prosecutor's opening speech

Unless the law involved in or the facts that support the charge are complicated, a prosecutor does not normally make an opening speech. If, however, he makes reference to the law involved, he must tell the magistrates all the law (Acts of Parliament, regulations, and decided cases) that is pertinent to the case, including that law which is adverse to his own case and helpful to the accused.

When the law is complicated, the prosecutor should itemise in clear and simple language each matter that he must prove before he has made out even a *prima facie* case against the accused and, if the prosecutor wishes to relate facts, he should state merely a précis of the evidence he will call, and not read his witnesses' statements in detail.

While making his opening speech, a prosecutor may refer to anything said by the accused but, in practice, unless he has a pertinent reason (other than a mere desire to gain a conviction) to do otherwise, a prosecutor is wise to omit any reference to anything said by the accused in case the defence argues and the Bench rules that what the accused said is inadmissible as evidence.

What a prosecutor states in his opening speech is not evidence and must never be treated as such by magistrates. At best, he states in his speech what he hopes to prove and this serves as a yardstick against which the testimony of the witnesses called should be measured: any material differences between the speech and the testimony of the witnesses should make a Bench suspicious of the testimony.

Prosecutors should be discouraged from making dramatic and colourful speeches. The purpose of a prosecutor's speech is to inform and not persuade a Bench.

Calling the prosecutor's witnesses

Those of the prosecutor's witnesses who are in court tell their story (having taken the oath or affirmed) from the witness box. Sometimes, witnesses are not required to testify in court, but instead have their statements read to the court (*see* page 63).

The wise advocate calls his witnesses to the box or reads their statements in sequence, the principal witness or complainant first, and thereafter the other witnesses in the order of the occurrence of the events they are testifying about.

Sometimes, a doctor has waiting patients or a police officer has been on night duty, and it is tempting for a prosecutor to call such witnesses out of sequence so they may get away from court. To do so is, however, unfair to the Bench and the accused: neither the Bench nor the accused have prior knowledge of the testimony that will be given by the prosecutor's witnesses and, if the story against the accused is not unfolded in an orderly manner, his advocate may omit some vital question.

Examination-in-Chief

Each witness, whether called by the prosecutor or the accused, is first questioned by the advocate who called him. That advocate must not ask the witness leading questions (*see* page 134).

Cross-examination

Next, the opposing advocate may question the witness.

He *must* question a witness about those parts of their testimony with which his client disagrees, since it is a general rule of law that when an advocate does not cross-examine a witness, he accepts as truthful the testimony of that witness. The questioning of a witness on those parts of his testimony that are not accepted is referred to as "Putting the accused's case". The prosecutor is also bound by the same rule.

The putting of questions need not be taken to ridiculous lengths. When a series of witnesses give similar evidence, an opposing advocate need not examine each of them in detail about those parts of their testimony which his client will refute. It is sufficient if the advocate indicates clearly to the Bench and the witness what it is that he does not accept.

As has been stated, there are occasions when the prosecutor calls witnesses out of the correct sequence, or in his opening speech fails to indicate with clarity his case against the accused. On such occasions, the accused's advocate cannot be criticised for failing to phrase his questions so as to "put the accused's case".

Although pompous and inexperienced advocates seldom lose an opportunity of cross-examining a witness, there are only two occasions when it is necessary:

(i) when the witness has said something his client will deny;

(ii) when the witness is thought to have information in addition to that which he has related.

The fact that an advocate omits to question a witness called by the other side does not indicate weakness in his client's case; it is merely that the testimony is accepted as true and such an omission is often an indication of strength.

A judge once said that cross-examination does not consist of examining crossly; a saying of which many advocates are ignorant. Nevertheless, there are occasions when an advocate needs to be severe and insistent with a deliberately recalcitrant, obstructive, or perverse witness and when a witness behaves in this manner the Bench should come to the advocate's aid. A Bench should also protect an accused and witnesses from a bullying and overbearing advocate. The roles of accused and witness are unhappy and often ignominious, and the search for the truth is seldom facilitated by frightening the accused or witnesses.

It is incorrect to say, as unrepresented accused are sometimes told, that the answer of a witness called by the other side must be accepted. So long as the same question is not repeated *ad nauseam*, it may be put to a witness more than once, although a subtle cross-examiner will rephrase, and thereby disguise, it. However, once an accused has denied an allegation little purpose is served by the prosecutor's repetition of his question or assertion in an increasingly belligerent tone.

It is emphasised, on the other hand, that an advocate must

accept the answer given by a witness whom he himself has called, unless he has the permission of the Bench to treat the witness as a hostile one.

During his opening speech, as stated earlier, the prosecutor ought to have set out his case against the accused and his questions to the accused and the accused's witnesses must be phrased with that case in mind.

A prosecutor who has failed to prove his case against the accused is not allowed to substitute another during the course of the trial.

Let us say the accused has been charged with exceeding a 30 m.p.h. speed limit, and the prosecutor's case is that the accused travelled at 70 m.p.h. During the trial it becomes obvious that the accused's speed was nothing like 70 m.p.h. So the prosecutor attempts to redirect his questions towards getting an admission from the accused that he had broken the law by travelling at 32 or 35 m.p.h. The prosecutor's case had been a highly dangerous 70 m.p.h., not a mere infringing 35 m.p.h. It is, therefore, improper to allow him to change his case.

Of course, if the accused admitted that he drove, or it was proved that he drove, at more than 30 m.p.h. the magistrates must convict the accused. The point is that the prosecutor may not change his case halfway through the trial merely to gain a conviction. If the prosecutor mentions a speed of 70 m.p.h. yet his witnesses can prove only a much lower speed, it is, as explained elsewhere, likely that the witnesses are lying and the magistrates should be suspicious of them.

Skilful and subtle cross-examination is always permissible and to be admired, but skill and subtlety must not become deceitful or misleading.

An accused's advocate must test the recollection and truthfulness of the prosecutor's witnesses, but he must not put to them a different version of the episode unless his client will later substantiate that different version on oath.

Similarly, a prosecutor must test the recollection and frankness of the accused and the accused's witnesses but, in so doing, he must not put to them a distorted version of their evidence or that given by anyone else.

It is the responsibility of the magistrates to ensure that the advocates behave fairly.

Re-examination

After the cross-examination, the advocate who called the witness may re-examine him.

When re-examining his witness, an advocate is severely limited in the range of his questions. He must:

(i)   not ask a leading question;

(ii) confine his questions to matters that were the subject of his opponent's cross-examination. (The advocate must not even touch on matters mentioned during his own examination-in-chief but not during cross-examination.)

The making of objections

As a result of ignorance, some advocates unnecessarily and improperly object to questions being asked by an opponent. Such objections are irritating to the court and the opponent when they are not justified. On the other hand, nothing is more galling for a competent advocate than to have his opponent disclose to the magistrates information by improper means, or information which cannot be classed as evidence. Not only is it galling to the advocate, but a judgment based on such information is an improper judgment.

There are occasions when making such objections leads to undignified arguments between the advocates and the purpose of the objection is then made all the more incomprehensible to the magistrates. Magistrates should therefore insist on the following procedure whenever an objection is made to a question or statement by an advocate, protracted as it may be:

1. When an opponent stands to make his objection, the examining advocate cuts short his question, sits and remains seated during the objection.

2. The objecting opponent states his objection.

3. The examining advocate replies to the objection.

4. Finally, the objector may be permitted to make a last speech.

An objection, to be valid, must be made hurriedly, but not discourteously. If the objection is not made quickly, the magistrates will be given the information even if the objection is well founded.

Information that is not evidence

There are occasions when magistrates need to hear information before they can decide whether or not it is admissible as evidence; a usual example is the whole or a part of a formal statement made by the accused.

Sometimes an accused objects to the magistrates being told of the contents of a statement which he made to the police because he made it as result of a threat or promise. The magistrates are in a quandary if, having heard of the circumstances surrounding the taking of the statement and the statement itself, they decide not to accept it as evidence. Inevitably, although they have ruled that the statement is not acceptable as evidence, the contents of the statement will have lodged in their minds and will influence their decision.

There is no emphatic rule as to what magistrates should do in such circumstances or when information is improperly related to them. Theoretically, there is no reason why they should not continue with the trial if they are confident that they can dismiss the information from their minds. However, in certain cases, such as where an accused's criminal record is wrongly introduced as evidence, magistrates would be wise to halt the trial and adjourn the issue to be tried by a fresh Bench, relying on the prosecutor not to re-introduce that information as evidence.

Indeed (although there is no rule of law that they must), magistrates to whom information is improperly related should always adjourn the case to be heard by a fresh Bench if that information is likely to influence their decision.

An advocate must object to improper information being given

to the magistrates. When deciding whether or not to uphold an objection, a magistrate should not take into consideration the fact that the particular piece of information would help him to decide the general issue of the case.

Questions by the court

With increasing frequency and severity, appeal courts are criticising professional judges who ask too many questions. Magistrates and their court clerks must heed this criticism, and ask only the absolute minimum of necessary questions, normally through the chairman.

When a chairman decides that it is proper for him to question a witness, he should delay doing so until the two advocates have finished with the witness. At the close of the chairman's questioning, both advocates should be given an opportunity to question the witness on the matters raised by the chairman; the advocate who called the witness questioning last.

Identifying the accused

Often, it is a necessary step in the prosecutor's case that the man who is being tried should be identified as the wrong-doer.

When the charge is one of dishonesty or involves physical violence, a formal identification parade at the police station is arranged. At such a parade, every effort is made by those in authority to ensure that the witness's recognition of the accused is based only on the accused's features and build. The accused may reject those whom he thinks are dissimilar to himself and choose his position in the line.

There are occasions, particularly in motoring cases, when the formal (and fair) identification parade is dispensed with, despite the fact that the identification of the accused, *e.g.* the driver of the offending car, is necessary to the prosecutor's case.

Instead the identification is made by asking the witness giving evidence to look around the court-room and say whether the wrong-doer is present.

Since the accused is in the dock or some other similarly isolated and prominent position, the witness will be well aware who is playing the role of the accused and will probably point to him, even if he does not actually recognise that person as the wrong-doer.

It is unfair that there should be two standards of identification or proof. Ideally any accused, whether motorist or not, whose identification is necessary to the prosecutor's case, should be given the protection of a formal identification parade.

Magistrates, although they may critically comment when there is no such parade, may not insist on there being one. Magistrates should insist on the identification in the court-room being as fair to the accused as possible by allowing the accused to position himself among the members of the public or in some other inconspicuous place in court.

Submission of "No Case to Answer"

The close of the prosecutor's case

When all his witnesses have testified, the prosecutor announces that he has closed his case against the accused.

At this moment the accused's advocate may submit that the prosecutor has failed to make out a case against the accused, *i.e.* that the accused has no case to answer.

Even if the accused's advocate does not make a submission, and particularly if the accused is unrepresented, the magistrates should mentally check that the prosecutor has proved all the essentials of the charge before allowing the trial to proceed.

The magistrates must dismiss the case if:

a) there has been no evidence that proves one or more of the essential elements in the alleged offence; or

b) the evidence adduced by the prosecutor has been so discredited as a result of cross-examination or is so manifestly unreliable that no reasonable tribunal could safely convict on it.

Furthermore, the magistrates must dismiss the charge at the close of the prosecutor's case if they are not clear what, specifically, the accused is supposed to have done wrong. This is a state of mind in which magistrates often find themselves at the end of a prosecutor's case in (but not only in) a "motor accident" prosecution.

Final submissions or submissions of "No Case to Answer"

At the end of the prosecutor's case in a criminal trial, the accused's advocate has two choices. He may submit that his client has no case to answer and, if the submission fails, call his evidence; or he may call no evidence at all and make his final submission.

When considering a submission of "No Case to Answer", the magistrates have to ensure only that:

a) the prosecutor has proved all the essentials required of him; and

b) the evidence called by the prosecutor is sufficiently believable to require the accused to answer it (tell his side of the story).

By the end of a trial, on the other hand, not only must the prosecutor have proved all the essentials required of him, but the magistrates, having heard both sides of the story, must be satisfied beyond all reasonable doubt that the prosecutor has proved the accused's guilt.

It follows that the occasions when an accused's advocate makes a final address at the close of the prosecutor's case (rather than make a submission of "No Case to Answer") are:

a) when he is so confident that the prosecutor has failed to make out a case against the accused that he is prepared to forgo his client's evidence (and, if necessary, appeal against an adverse verdict);

b) when there is some doubt as to whether the prosecutor has made out a case against the accused, but (because he knows that the accused may make damaging replies to the cross-examination) he dare not put the accused in the witness box;

c) when he thinks that the prosecutor has just made out a *prima facie* case, yet has not proved the accused's guilt beyond all reasonable doubt.

If, at the close of a submission of "No Case to Answer" which they reject, the magistrates say more than "We find that there is a case to answer", they may be giving the accused grounds either to insist on the case being retried before another Bench of magistrates or to appeal to a higher court.

For the sake of clarity, when an accused's advocate makes a speech at the close of the prosecutor's case, the chairman of the Bench should ask, "Are you:

a) making an opening address;

b) making a submission of "No Case to Answer"; or

c) making a final address with the intention of *not* calling witnesses no matter what is our decision?"

Procedure on a submission of "No Case to Answer"

1. The accused's advocate indicates that he wishes to make a submission.

2. The chairman of the Bench asks what is the nature of the submission.

3. The accused's advocate submits that:

a) according to the law (Acts of Parliament, regulations, and decided cases);

b) on the evidence called by the prosecutor; or

c) both according to the law and on the evidence called by the prosecutor,

the prosecutor has either failed to make out any case against the accused or has failed to make out a case on which a reasonable tribunal could safely convict the accused.

4. The prosecutor may reply if, and only if, there was a reference to the law in the submission of the accused's advocate. Even then, the prosecutor must confine his reply to legal arguments, and not touch on references to or criticisms of the quality, truth, or possibility of his evidence.

5. The accused's advocate may answer the prosecutor's reply.

Whether as a result of their own deliberations or following a submission of "No Case to Answer", the magistrates decide that the accused has no case to answer, they must dismiss the charge.

Even if the magistrates decide that the accused has a case to answer, they are still a very long way from finding that the accused is guilty. The accused is still an innocent man, and the burden is still on the prosecutor to prove the accused's guilt beyond all reasonable doubt. Magistrates must not feel that, because they have decided that the accused has a case to answer, they are apparently changing their minds or losing face if they subsequently acquit him.

Omissions by the prosecutor

Occasionally, a prosecutor fails to prove some essential element of his case and realises his failure either before the accused starts to give evidence or later in the trial.

Magistrates have the authority to allow a prosecutor to prove a forgotten but essential element although he has closed his case, but that authority should be exercised judicially.

If the prosecutor has failed to prove a mere, although essential, formality (such as his authority to prosecute) he should readily be given permission to remedy the defect in his case. If the defect is more fundamental or, more particularly, if subsequent evidence has reminded a prosecution witness of his failure to give an essential piece of testimony, permission to remedy the defect in the prosecutor's case should reluctantly and rarely be given and certainly should not be given after the Bench have retired to consider their verdict. Indeed, there are many who consider it should not be given after the defence has closed its case.

Opening speech for the defence

Before calling his evidence, the accused's advocate may make an opening speech. The accused's advocate is under no obligation to make such a speech and is unlikely to make it unless the defence is so complicated that it might be difficult for the magistrates to follow and appreciate it without the speech.

Should the accused's advocate decide that it is necessary to make an opening speech, the following three rules apply:

1. The accused or his advocate may not make a second speech at the close of all the evidence unless he has called to the witness box the accused and at least one other witness, although, presumably the testimony of that second witness could be in written statement form (*see* page 63).

2. Even then, he may make the second speech only if the Bench gives him permission to do so.

3. If the accused or his advocate is allowed that second speech, the prosecutor may, as of right, make a speech at the close of all the evidence. The prosecutor must make his speech before the accused or his advocate makes his second speech.

Thus, during a summary trial of a criminal offence, the accused or his advocate is always entitled to make the last speech.

Should an accused's advocate make an opening speech, it is usual for the Bench to allow him to make a second speech if he asks permission to do so. But before he launches into that second speech, the court clerk should courteously interrupt him to inquire of the prosecutor whether he wishes to make a speech at this stage.

Calling the accused and his witnesses

Next, the defence calls its evidence.

The accused must be the first to testify and, thereafter, his witnesses should be called to the witness box in some definite order.

The accused and his witnesses are:

   (i) examined-in-chief by the accused's advocate;

   (ii) cross-examined by the prosecutor;

   (iii) re-examined by the accused's advocate.

During these examinations, the same rules apply as when the prosecutor's witnesses were giving evidence.

Rebutting evidence

At the close of the accused's case, *i.e.* when the accused and his witnesses have given their evidence, the prosecutor may call witnesses to rebut the accused's case.

The occasions when rebutting evidence may be called are rare. Rebutting evidence may be called only when, during the accused's case, some matter arose which no human ingenuity on the part of the prosecutor could have foreseen.

Furthermore, rebutting evidence must be strictly confined to rebutting the accused's defence and not directed to bolstering up the prosecutor's case.

Witnesses called to rebut the accused's case are:

(i) examined-in-chief by the prosecutor;

(ii) cross-examined by the accused's advocate;

(iii) re-examined by the prosecutor.

Proof by written statement

In any criminal proceedings, other than committal proceedings, a written statement made by any person (other than a person under ten years of age), shall, if such of the conditions hereafter mentioned as are applicable are satisfied, be admissible as evidence to the same extent as oral evidence given by that person.

The right to introduce written statements applies only to criminal (not to civil, domestic, or administrative) proceedings before the magistrates. Although written statements may be introduced at committal proceedings (*see* page 94), the procedure is different from that applicable to summary trials, which is outlined here.

The conditions that must be satisfied before a written statement may be accepted as evidence at a summary trial are:

a) the statement purports to be signed by the person who made it;

b) the statement contains a declaration by that person to the effect that:

(i) it is true to the best of his knowledge and belief;

(ii) he made the statement knowing that, if it were tendered in evidence, he would be liable to prosecution if he wilfully stated in it anything which he knew to be false or did not believe to be true (written statements of persons under ten years of age may not be admitted as evidence, because persons under that age may not be held to be criminally responsible);

c) before the hearing at which the statement is tendered in evidence, a copy of the statement is served by or on behalf of the party proposing to tender it on:

(i) as soon as is practicable, the clerk to the justices;

(ii) each of the other parties to the proceedings (even on those who are unaffected by the contents of the statement);

d) none of the other parties or their solicitors, within seven days from the service of the copy of the statement serves notice on the party proposing to tender the statement, objecting to the statement being tendered in evidence.

The conditions mentioned in paragraphs (c) and (d) need not be observed so long as all the parties agree either before or during the hearing.

Whenever a written statement is tendered instead of the witness testifying in person:

a) if the statement is made by a person under the age of twenty-one, it shall give his age;

b) if it is made by a person who cannot read, it shall be read to him before he signs it and shall be accompanied by a declaration by the person who read the statement to the effect that it was so read;

c) if it refers to any other document as an exhibit, the copy served on the clerk to the justices and any other party to the proceedings shall be accompanied by a copy of that document or by such information as may be necessary in order to enable the party on whom it is served to inspect that document or a copy.

Although a written statement may have been correctly prepared and served and no party to the proceedings has objected prior to the hearing to its introduction as evidence, at the hearing the party on whose behalf the statement was served may call the witness to give oral evidence. Furthermore, the court on the application of any party to the proceedings may require the maker of the statement to testify orally.

Any party to the proceedings may, subject to complying with the conditions, introduce a written statement as evidence. During a summary trial, however, only the prosecutor is likely to avail himself of the procedure. This is because the accused and his advisers are ignorant of the prosecutor's case until the trial is well under way. Not until the prosecutor's case is closed can the accused's advocate plan in detail the information he must try to extract from his own client and his witnesses.

The fact that a written statement is introduced as evidence does not mean that all of it is automatically accepted as evidence; should any of it be inadmissible as evidence (because, for instance, that part offended the hearsay rule), that part must be ignored by the Bench. The chairman is required to mark the written statement "Ruled inadmissible .... Justice of the Peace".

The admissible parts of the statement must be read aloud in court by or on behalf of the party tendering it, unless the court otherwise directs. In this event an oral account must be given of the parts not read aloud.

It is not easy to listen intelligently when someone reads a statement aloud, yet magistrates must ensure that they hear and understand the purport of everything read to them. If the Bench is doubtful about anything of importance in a statement, they should insist on the witness being brought to court to testify orally, rather than accepting an advocate's explanation (after all, if an orally testifying witness is not understood, he is questioned until what he says is understood; an advocate is not permitted to say, "What he means is ....").

The fact that an accused or other party to the proceedings does not object to the introduction of a written statement, instead of causing the witness to attend court, means that the accused or other party is admitting the truth of what the statement contains.

False written statements tendered in evidence

It is an offence for a witness to "wilfully make a statement material in these proceedings which he knows to be false or does not believe to be true".

Proof by formal admission

Subject to safeguards, any fact of which oral evidence may be given in any criminal proceedings may be admitted by or on behalf of the prosecutor or accused. Once such a fact is admitted, it is conclusive evidence in those particular proceedings against the party who made the admission.

An admission may be made before or during the proceedings.

If the admission is not made in court it must be in writing and, if made by an individual, must be signed by him; while if it is made by a body corporate, it must be signed by a director, secretary or manager of, or clerk to, the corporate body.

When the admission is made during the proceedings, it must be written down and signed by or on behalf of the person making it.

Magistrates are wise to ensure that admissions, particularly those made during a trial, are precise and clear. It is embarrassing for everyone if, later in the trial, there is a dispute as to what was admitted.

The law states that an admission made by an individual before the trial should be approved by his counsel or solicitor who, presumably, may withdraw or amend the admission. It also states that an admission "made on behalf of a defendant who is an individual, shall be made by his counsel or solicitor".

A formal admission may, with the leave of the court, be withdrawn in the proceedings for the purpose of which it was made or at any subsequent criminal proceedings relating to the same matter.

The final speech

As was stated earlier, it is unusual for an accused's advocate to make an opening speech and, therefore, the accused's is usually the only advocate to make a speech at the close of the case.

During his final speech, the accused's advocate may argue that in law his client is not guilty. He may emphasise those parts of the law that favour his contention, but he must not misquote the law or mislead the magistrates as to what is the law.

He may stress the parts of and omissions from the evidence that favour his client and draw the magistrates' attention to any inconsistencies in that evidence. He must not, of course, distort or mislead the magistrates as to what was said.

He must remember also that he is an advocate and not a witness. He must base his arguments on only the evidence given during the trial; he may not introduce new information.

To this final speech the magistrates should listen with great attention and wholly open minds.

Unless the accused's advocate made an opening speech, the prosecutor is not entitled to make a speech at this stage even if the accused's advocate referred to legal matters in his closing speech. So long as the accused's advocate does not misquote the law or the evidence, the prosecutor may not reply or object to any inferences that the accused's advocate puts on the law or facts or conclusions he asks the magistrates to draw from those inferences.

The magistrates' deliberation

Only at this moment may a magistrate start deciding whether the accused is innocent or guilty; until this moment he must consider the accused innocent.

The balances

Magistrates may convict the accused only if:

    (i)   they are aware what is the prosecutor's case against the accused; and

    (ii) where they differ, they prefer the prosecutor's witnesses to those of the accused; and

(iii) they prefer the prosecutor's to the accused's legal arguments; and

(iv) the prosecutor has proved each and every element of the offence that he is required to prove; and

(v) they are satisfied that the prosecutor has proved the accused's guilt beyond all reasonable doubt.

Should the magistrates decide any one of these five matters against the prosecutor, the accused must be acquitted.

Should the magistrates find that they cannot accept either the prosecutor's story and contention or those of the accused, they must acquit the accused.

Equally, the magistrates must acquit the accused if they find that they believe both the opposing stories and contentions (in other words, if they cannot make up their minds whom to believe).

Reasonable doubt

All too often, a magistrate's state of indecision is greater than a mere inability to prefer one story to another: often, the magistrate is of the opinion that the accused may be guilty, but is not certain that he is. When this is so, the magistrate must remember that before the accused may be convicted, the prosecutor must have proved the accused's guilt beyond all reasonable doubt.

A magistrate need not be "dead certain" of an accused's guilt before conviction: since all of us can conjure up imaginary or foolish doubts about a man's guilt, there would be few convictions if magistrates had to be dead certain before they could convict.

A magistrate should decide whether an accused is innocent or guilty with the same common sense that he uses when he approaches family, household, or business problems.

When a magistrate has sensible doubts as to the accused's guilt, he must opt for acquittal. If magistrates have doubts as to the accused's guilt, they must not resolve those doubts by convicting and then passing a ridiculous or inappropriately light sentence: to do so is dishonest.

Extraneous information

Occasionally, information that has an emotional or otherwise improper effect on the magistrates is introduced, even though it does not help to prove or disprove the allegation under consideration. At the time, it is not always possible to recognise that such information is not evidence, but magistrates must ensure that their final decision is not based on anything other than evidence that directly proves or disproves the issue.

For instance, during a case of driving without due care and attention, it does not help the magistrates to decide the guilt or innocence of the accused to be told that someone was injured in the accident because:

a) a motorist may drive most dangerously, yet collide with no one;

b) another motorist's fault may amount to a mere triviality, yet, as a result of it, a third party may be maimed for life;

c) a pedestrian may "commit suicide" by carelessly walking into the side of a vehicle that is being properly driven.

The relative values of witnesses

A police officer or other witness has no special value merely because he happens to be in uniform or called by the prosecutor. Neither have the accused and his witnesses a lower value merely because he is the accused and his witnesses are called by him. The magistrates should assume that everyone who steps into the witness box will speak the truth, until it is proved otherwise.

The danger of generalities

When deciding on their verdict, the magistrates must forget everything that has not been introduced as evidence during the trial and the comments of the advocates on that evidence. Certainly, they must beware of making assumptions; the mere fact that, for instance, the police have decided to prosecute the accused is no indication that the accused "must have done wrong".

Finally, the upbringing and social background of an accused and the witnesses often determines their behaviour, modes of speech and reactions. Magistrates should bear this in mind when evaluating their truthfulness.

Magistrates and their fellow magistrates

When they retire to consider their verdict, a Bench of magistrates may discuss the evidence and their thoughts on the case and may, when there are more than two magistrates present, act on a majority vote. Nevertheless, each magistrate must make his own decision and the final verdict is the personal responsibility of each member of the Bench.

The chairman of the Bench has no second or casting vote, but should control his fellow magistrates' deliberations and voting, ensuring that nothing extraneous enters the discussion.

Obviously, the magistrates will listen with care to what their colleagues say, and will state their own views. In the end, however, a magistrate who is:

a) convinced of the accused's innocence; or

b) not certain beyond all reasonable doubt of the accused's guilt,

must adamantly maintain his decision and vote for an acquittal, even if he is in the minority.

Similarly, a magistrate who is soberly and properly convinced of the accused's guilt is true to his judicial oath if he votes for a conviction.

When two magistrates only are trying a case, a disagreement between them as to the verdict necessitates the case being tried again by another Bench. Some magistrates, quite wrongly, are reluctant to be the cause of a second trial; in fact, a magistrate who, having properly and judicially made his decision, maintains it, is to be admired. If, however, there is to be a compromise, it must be the magistrate favouring a conviction who gives way.

Where there is more than one charge against the accused or there are two or more accused being tried together, a separate verdict must be reached in respect of each charge and each accused. The fact that the verdict on one charge is "Not Guilty" does not necessarily mean that the accused is innocent of all the charges, nor does the conviction of one accused necessarily mean that the others are guilty.

A magistrate can act judicially only if he is confident that any quarrels or disputes that may take place in the privacy of the magistrates' retiring room will not later be the subject of amused and critical comment. Therefore, no matter how vehemently a Bench may argue and disagree over a decision, what was said should be forgotten and remain secret once the decision is reached.

The verdict

When there is more than one charge, the chairman of the Bench should prepare a list of all the charges and the verdicts before returning to the court. Should there be two or more accused, separate lists are required for each one. It is sometimes advisable for the chairman to tell the court clerk of the verdicts before announcing them, in case the magistrates have, for instance, wrongly paired off two alternative charges.

Finally, without comment, the chairman should announce the verdict of "Guilty" or "Not Guilty" in respect of each charge and each accused.

When the verdict is "Not Guilty", the accused leaves the court a free man.

A request by an acquitted accused for costs

An acquitted accused may ask that he be awarded the costs of his defence. Such costs include both the pre-trial taking of statements from the accused and witnesses and the general preparation for the trial, and the actual presentation of the defence in court.

The mere fact that an accused has been acquitted is not, in itself, a reason why he should be awarded his costs. The magistrates have a discretion, which they must exercise judicially, whether or not the accused should be paid his costs.

It should be noted that costs in respect of offences triable either way are payable out of Central Funds (*see* page 44). Costs in relation to offences which can only be tried summarily are payable as between the parties. Although the award of costs must always remain a matter for the court's discretion, in the light of the circumstances of the particular case, it should be accepted as normal practice that when the court has power to award costs out of Central Funds it should do so in favour of a successful accused unless there are positive reasons for making a different order.

In the case of an accused who is in receipt of legal aid, the magistrates will not make an order for costs from Central Funds.

If the magistrates decide to grant an accused the costs of his defence, they make an order to that effect.

An order that an acquitted accused's costs should be paid by the prosecutor or from public funds would be appropriate when, for example:

a) the prosecutor, patently, never had a case against the accused;

b) had the prosecution exercised reasonable foresight and made proper and full inquiries, it would have anticipated the form of the accused's defence and its success; or

c) from the outset the accused was wholly frank, yet the prosecution chose to disbelieve him;

d) where the prosecution has acted spitefully or without reasonable cause. Here the defendant's own costs should be paid by the prosecutor. Where the defendant's own conduct has brought suspicion on himself and has misled the prosecution into thinking that the case against him is stronger than it really is, then the defendant should pay his own costs; or

e) where there is ample evidence to support a verdict of guilty but the defendant is entitled to an acquittal on account of some procedural difficulty. Here the defendant may be safely left to pay his own costs.

Costs when charge dismissed or withdrawn

As stated on page 47, there are occasions when a charge is dismissed for want of prosecution or withdrawn by the prosecutor.

If the charge against him has been dismissed or withdrawn, an accused may be awarded costs from Central Funds, provided the charge was in respect of an offence triable either way (*see* page 44).

The sentence

After a finding of guilt the magistrates must decide and announce any penalty they inflict on the accused in respect of each offence.

The finality

That is the end of the trial. The magistrate who has been patient, attentive and, where necessary, sympathetic or severe; who has ensured that the rules of evidence and trial have been obeyed by everyone, including himself; who has based his verdict only on admissible evidence; and who has had the courage to be judicially independent has been true to his judicial oath. He is wise to forget the trial and certainly should not discuss it with anyone, whether or not that person was a party to it.

CHAPTER 5

SENTENCING ADULT OFFENDERS

Procedure

After a finding of guilt, the usual procedure is:

a) the chairman or the court clerk publicly asks whether:

   (i) the offender has any previous convictions;

   (ii) whether the prosecutor is asking that the offender be ordered to pay or contribute towards any costs or expenses or to pay an aggrieved person compensation;

b) the offender or his advocate is invited to address the Bench in mitigation of sentence and to comment on any application for costs or expenses that the prosecutor may have made;

c) after conferring with his colleagues on the Bench, the chairman announces the sentence.

Homilies

The wise chairman states the sentence firmly and baldly and does not deliver a homily to the offender or a vindication of the conviction or the sentence. A homily delivered at this moment rarely has any influence on an offender, who is either too indifferent or too afraid to pay attention, whereas newspapers regard homilies and vindications as excellent copy. In any event, very few, even professional, judges have the necessary histrionic ability to make what they say at this stage sound worthwhile and nothing sounds more foolish than an ill-thought out, ill-delivered stricture.

The general principles

When deciding on the sentence, there are five, at least, matters that the magistrates must bear in mind:

1. The offender must not be additionally punished because his defence necessitated the searching cross-examination

74

of a child, frail old person, police officer, or other of the prosecutor's witnesses.

2. No matter how long winded, rude, inept or exasperating the offender's advocate may have been, the offender must not be additionally punished because of his choice of advocate.

3. The magistrates must ignore events over which the offender had no control. For instance, the fact that a crowd interfered and hampered the police while the offender was being arrested is something that should be ignored, unless, of course, the offender incited the crowd.

4. Magistrates must ignore possible criticism of their verdict and sentence from their acquaintances and the newspapers.

5. The offender is an individual, and although the public must be protected and potential wrong-doers dissuaded from crime, the offender's sentence must be based on his previous innocence or wrongdoings and the circumstances surrounding the offence for which he is to be sentenced.

The Criminal Justice Act 1991 set out three main ways of dealing with an offender, according to the seriousness of the offence. At the lower end of the scale there are offences which a Bench feels can reasonably be dealt with either by a discharge or by way of a financial penalty. The next group comprises offences the circumstances of which lead magistrates to conclude that they are serious enough to warrant a community sentence. Finally, there are those offences which the court considers to be so serious that only a custodial sentence is appropriate.

The Act also, somewhat controversially, changed the way in which previous convictions may be considered. Section 29 of the Act sought to give effect to the principle that the sentence of the court should relate to the present offence and its seriousness, not an offender's record, nor his failure to respond to previous sentences, and that a previous conviction should only have a bearing if the *circumstances* of that earlier conviction are an aggravating factor. However, there was considerable disquiet about this aspect of the Act and it was repealed in the Criminal Justice Act 1993.

Discharges: absolute and conditional

When the magistrates are of the opinion, having regard to the circumstances (including the nature of the offence and the character of the offender) that:

a) it is inexpedient to inflict punishment;

b) a probation or community order is not appropriate,

they may discharge the offender either absolutely or conditionally.

An absolute discharge

When, taking everything into consideration, the magistrates do not think it appropriate to punish the offender in any way or, even, to ask him not to misbehave in future, they should discharge the offender absolutely. An absolute discharge means that the offender has been convicted, but for certain purposes it does not rank as a conviction.

A conditional discharge

Again, taking everything into consideration, the magistrates may decide not to inflict punishment on an offender but think it wise to put some measure of restraint on him. If so, they may discharge the offender conditionally; that is, the discharge is subject to a condition that the offender does not commit another offence during the following period specified by the magistrates. This period may not exceed three years.

Should the offender be convicted of a further offence during that specified period, he is liable to be punished for the offence in respect of which he was conditionally discharged.

A conditional discharge differs from a Probation Order (*see* page 79) in that the only condition that may be imposed when an offender is discharged conditionally is that he will not commit another offence during the specified period. A conditionally discharged offender is not put under any form of supervision.

Fines

Magistrates may impose a fine of any amount up to the maximum specified in the statute creating the offence. Before fixing the amount of any fine, a court must take into account, so far as they are known, the financial circumstances of the offender and the amount must also be such as, in the opinion of the court, reflects the seriousness of the offence.

A warrant of commitment

A Bench of magistrates may not fine an offender *and* at the same time either issue a warrant of commitment for default in payment or fix an alternative term of imprisonment on the occasion of conviction unless:

a) in the case of an offence punishable with imprisonment, the offender appears to the magistrates to have sufficient means to pay the fine forthwith; or

b) it appears to the court that the offender is unlikely to remain long enough at a place of abode in the United Kingdom to enable payment of the sum to be enforced by other methods; or

c) on the occasion of conviction, the offender is sentenced to immediate imprisonment or is already serving a term of imprisonment.

When a warrant of commitment is not issued forthwith, it cannot be issued at a later date unless the offender is already serving a term of imprisonment or the court has inquired into his means on at least one occasion in his presence.

Where there has been an inquiry into the means of the offender, the court may not on the occasion of the inquiry issue a warrant unless:

a) the offence is punishable with imprisonment and the offender appears to have the means to pay forthwith; or

b) all other means of enforcement have been tried or considered and are unsuccessful or appear to be inappropriate.

Presence of a defaulter required

After an offender has been convicted by a Magistrates' Court, the court cannot issue a warrant of commitment or fix a term in default of payment except at a hearing at which the offender is present, but this does not apply where the court has already issued a suspended commitment under the powers set out above (*"A warrant of commitment"*) or the offender is already serving a term of imprisonment.

The hearing at which the offender is present may be either a means inquiry or a special hearing called for the purpose and in both cases the provisions of the Magistrates' Courts Act relating to the issue of summonses and warrants to bring the offender to court, will apply.

Means statement

Either before or on inquiring into an offender's means, a magistrate may require the offender to fill in a statement of his means. It is an offence for an offender to refuse to give the statement or to deliberately or recklessly give wrong or inadequate material information.

Remission of fines

On a means inquiry subsequent to a conviction by a Magistrates' Court, the same court (though not necessarily the same magistrates) may remit the whole or any part of the fine if it thinks it just to do so having regard to any change in the offender's circumstances since the conviction. Any term of imprisonment already fixed must be reduced proportionately to the amount of fine remitted.

Community sentences

The range of community orders which may be included in a community sentence is as follows:

a Probation Order;

a Community Service Order;

a Combination Order;

a Curfew Order;

an Attendance Centre Order.

A Pre-Sentence Report must be obtained before a Probation Order, Community Service Order or Combination Order is made.

Before passing a community sentence, the magistrates must be satisfied that the offence is serious enough to warrant such a sentence.

Probation Order

Instead of punishing an offender in another way, a Magistrates' Court may make a Probation Order in respect of an offender where, having regard to the circumstances, including:

a) the nature of the offence; and

b) the character of the offender,

the court is of the opinion that a Probation Order is appropriate.

A Probation Order should be made if it is desirable in the interests of securing the rehabilitation of the offender, protecting the public from harm or preventing the commission of further offences.

A Probation Order's duration may not be less than six months, nor longer than three years.

During the period of the order, the offender is under the supervision of a probation officer. In addition, the order may be so phrased as to require the offender to comply with such other requirements as the court, having regard to all the circumstances of the case, considers to be necessary to secure his good conduct and prevent him from committing more offences.

Requirements that are often made of accused persons include:

a) that the offender shall report to and be visited by his probation officer;

b) that the offender shall tell his probation officer of changes in his residence and employment;

c) that the offender shall lead an industrious and honest life.

Additional requirements that may be included in the Probation Order include conditions as to residence, activities, attendance at a probation centre, treatment for a mental condition and treatment for drug or alcohol dependencies.

Provision is also made for longer and more intensive supervision of offenders who are given Probation Orders for sexual offences.

Whatever are the requirements of a Probation Order, the chairman or the court clerk (and it is usually preferable that it should be the court clerk) must explain them to the offender in layman's terms. The offender must also be told that, should he be convicted of a further offence during the term of the Probation Order, he is liable to be sentenced for the offence in respect of which he is, now, being placed on probation as well as in respect of the further offence.

An offender must agree:

    a) to being placed on probation;

    b) to the particular requirements applicable to him.

Should he refuse to agree to comply with those requirements, the Bench must decide on some other way of dealing with him.

If, during the term of a Probation Order, it appears to the magistrates that probation is no longer appropriate because the probationer cannot effectively be supervised, the magistrates may substitute for the Probation Order a conditional discharge for the unexpired term of the Probation Order.

When a probationer is brought before the magistrates for failing to comply with his Probation Order, the magistrates may:

    a) fine the probationer, in which case the Probation Order will continue to be effective for the balance of its term; or

    b) sentence the probationer for the offence in respect of which he was put on probation, in which case the Probation Order ceases.

Community Service Order

Magistrates have the power with this order to make offenders carry out unpaid work for the benefit of the community. It is intended to be used where a significant restriction of liberty is considered appropriate.

The order combines a means of imposing the sanction of deprivation of leisure time with the idea of putting back something into the community against which the offence was committed.

Schemes are available all over the country and offenders may be ordered to perform community service if they are considered suitable in a Pre-Sentence Report prepared by a probation officer.

The scheme's organising officer specifies and supervises work to be carried out. Such schemes include work on constructing a community centre, building adventure playgrounds, gardening in old persons homes and assisting the disabled and handicapped. The maximum number of hours is two hundred and forty and the minimum forty hours.

There are powers to bring a person who is in breach of a Community Service Order back before the court, in which case a fine may be imposed and the order allowed to continue, or the order revoked and the offender re-sentenced in some other way for the original offence.

Combination Order

This order combines the elements of both probation and community service. It can be combined with other community orders or with financial penalties if thought necessary.

The order is intended for offenders who magistrates believe should make some reparation to the community through a Community Service Order and who also need probation to tackle problems that underline the offending.

The maximum duration of the probation element of the order is three years and the minimum twelve months. The minimum number of community service hours is forty hours. The idea behind the order is that probation should continue for at least as long as community service work is being performed.

Curfew Order

This order compels offenders to be at the place specified in the order for the period of time specified. This will normally be the offender's place of residence and the order can be electronically monitored if the magistrates so decide. The maximum number of hours in a day in which the curfew can operate is twelve hours and the minimum is two hours. Such an order cannot operate for more than six months. At the time of writing, the provision for electronic monitoring is not in use.

Different places, days and lengths of time for different days can be specified within the order to take into account the circumstances of the offender.

Attendance Centre Order

Such an order may be made for any offender under the age of twenty-one:

a) convicted of an offence punishable with imprisonment; or

b) who has failed to comply with the requirements of a Probation Order.

When making the order magistrates must state the total number of hours the offender must be at the Attendance Centre. The total may be anything from twelve to thirty-six hours and is usually made up of periods of two hours spread over the appropriate number of Saturday afternoons.

Young Offenders Institutions

In the case of a male offender who is at least eighteen and under twenty-one and who has been convicted of an offence for which, had he been an adult, he could have been sent to prison, the magistrates may order him to a Young Offenders Institution (formerly known as either a Detention Centre or Borstal).

The magistrates may not sentence a person aged at least eighteen and under twenty-one to a Young Offenders Institution unless they are satisfied that there is no other appropriate method of dealing with him. In other words, the Bench must have considered one or other of the discharges, a fine, probation, an Attendance Centre Order or a community sentence, and rejected them all as inappropriate. Since such persons must not lightly be given such a sentence, magistrates must publicly state their reasons for taking this course when they do so.

Imprisonment

A Magistrates' Court may not sentence an offender to prison unless the statute that creates the offence of which he was convicted so permits. Even if the statute makes the offence punishable with imprisonment, there are certain restrictions on the sending of an offender to prison to which the magistrates must have regard. The magistrates may not sentence a first offender over the age of twenty-one to prison unless they are of the opinion that no other method of dealing with the offender is appropriate. Again, should a Bench decide that it must send a first offender to prison, it must state its reason for so doing. (A first offender is a person who has not been convicted of an offence that is punishable with imprisonment since he was eighteen.)

Restrictions on custodial sentencing of persons not legally represented

Magistrates may not send to prison or a Young Offenders Institution for the first time any person who is not legally represented in court unless:

(i) the accused had a legal aid application refused because his means were too great; or

(ii) where the accused had been told of his rights, he refused representation or failed to apply for legal aid.

Suspended sentences

The fact that magistrates sentence an offender to imprisonment does not necessarily mean that he immediately or, in fact, ever goes to prison. This is because when any court passes a sentence of two years' or less imprisonment it may, in certain limited circumstances, suspend the sentence.

When passing the sentence, the magistrates must fix and announce the period of the suspension (the "operational period") which must be of at least one year's and not more than two years' duration.

The power to suspend does not apply to sentences to a Young Offenders Institution. These sentences take immediate effect.

When an offender is being dealt with for two or more offences and is sentenced to a suspended period of imprisonment on each of two or more of the offences, the magistrates must make it clear whether the sentences are to run concurrently or consecutively. A court may not impose a suspended sentence of imprisonment in respect of one offence and place the offender on probation for another offence at the same time.

When passing a suspended sentence, the court (preferably the clerk) must explain to the offender in ordinary language what will happen to him if he is convicted of an offence punishable with imprisonment during the operational period (*see below*).

What courts can deal with an offender during his operational period

Suspended sentence passed by Magistrates' Court

When the suspended sentence was passed by a Magistrates' Court and the offender is convicted by the same or another Magistrates' Court of an offence punishable with imprisonment and committed during the operational period of the suspended sentence, the second Magistrates' Court, without having to obtain the consent of the first, may deal with the offender for the suspended sentence as well as for the further offence.

Suspended sentence passed by Crown Court

When the suspended sentence was passed by the Crown Court and the offender is convicted by a Magistrates' Court of an offence punishable with imprisonment and committed during the operational period of the suspended sentence, the magistrates will normally commit the offender in custody or on bail to the Crown Court which imposed the suspended sentence but, having regard to the time when and the place where the offender is likely to be dealt with, they may commit the offender to some other more appropriate Crown Court, so long as he will not thereby suffer hardship.

Magistrates will normally commit a person whom they convict of an offence punishable with imprisonment during his operational period to the appropriate Crown Court but they are not bound to do so; it is at their discretion.

When a Magistrates' Court decides not to commit an offender to the Crown Court, it must give written notice of the conviction of the offender during his operational period to the clerk of the Crown Court that imposed the suspended sentence. That Crown Court can then decide whether or not it wants to have the offender brought before it to be dealt with.

Discovery of further offences

When it appears to a judge or magistrate on whom jurisdiction is conferred that an offender has been convicted of an offence punishable with imprisonment and committed during the operational period of a suspended sentence and has not been dealt with in respect of the suspended sentence, he may issue a summons or warrant to bring the offender before the court.

One way in which a higher court will probably gain this information is by a notice from a Magistrates' Court, when a Bench has exercised its discretion not to commit the offender to the appropriate higher court. In all probability, however, these are the occasions when higher courts will not think it necessary to have the offenders brought before them.

Although a Magistrates' Court which convicts an offender of an offence punishable with imprisonment which was committed during his operational period may, at the same time, deal with the offender for the suspended sentence even if another Magistrates' Court passed the suspended sentence, only a magistrate of the Magistrates' Court which passed the suspended sentence may issue a summons or warrant for this purpose.

The application for a warrant must be in writing and on oath.

Powers of the magistrates when dealing with suspended sentences

When a Bench of magistrates is dealing with an offender for an offence punishable with imprisonment and that offence was committed during the operational period of a suspended sentence imposed by a Magistrates' Court, the Bench may deal with the offender in respect of the suspended sentence by one of the following methods; that is, the Bench may:

a) order that the suspended sentence shall take effect immediately, unaltered, unless it is of the opinion that it would be unjust in view of all the circumstances which have arisen since the suspended sentence was imposed, including the facts of the subsequent offence (and where the Bench is of that opinion, it must state its reasons);

b) order that the suspended sentence shall take effect immediately, but for a reduced term of imprisonment;

c) vary the original order by suspending the sentence for a further period which must not exceed two years; or

d) make no order (which counts as "dealing" with the offender in respect of the suspended sentence).

As a general rule, when magistrates order that a suspended sentence shall take effect, the suspended sentence should run consecutively to any sentence of imprisonment to which the magistrates may at that time sentence the accused.

Deferment of sentence

The magistrates have power to defer passing sentence on an offender after conviction for a single specified period not exceeding six months. The object of this provision is to enable the court better to select the appropriate sentence and to take into account his conduct after some unexpected change in circumstances, *e.g.* obtaining employment or subsequent marriage. The offender's consent to deferment is required.

At the end of the period, a progress report on the offender from a probation officer may be required by the court.

It should be stressed that this deferment is merely postponement of the sentencing itself.

Once there has been a deferment of a sentence, magistrates have no power to commit an offender to the Crown Court.

CHAPTER 6

CRIMINAL JURISDICTION: COMMITTAL COURT

Before an accused is required to stand his trial at the Crown Court he must have been committed thereto by an ordinary magistrate presiding over a committal court. In this role, a magistrate is referred to as an examining justice.

The five procedures

There are five types of committal proceedings over which a magistrate may be required to preside. They are:

1. The "paper" (sometimes referred to as a "section 6(2)") committal, when the examining magistrate is not required even to read the papers.

2. The "read out" committal, when the witnesses do not attend and testify on oath in court but, instead, their testimony is read to the court.

3. The "oral" committal (sometimes referred to as an "old style" committal), when all the witnesses are required to attend and testify in court.

4. The "part oral" committal, when some witnesses are required to attend and testify in court, while the testimony of other witnesses is read to the court.

5. When, as in a summary trial (*see* page 66), an accused admits facts, and the balance of the evidence is related orally and/or read from written statements.

The accused has the final choice of procedure

From the magistrates' and court clerk's points of view, "paper" committal is best; most of the typing has already been done by those responsible for the prosecution, the committal may be fitted into any court list, the procedure takes no more than ten minutes and the Bench has no decision to make.

For this reason, clerks to magistrates encourage the adoption of the section 6(2) procedure whenever possible. However, there are occasions when a defence advocate prefers that the prosecutor's witnesses should attend court and testify: perhaps he wishes to test the quality of those witnesses; perhaps he believes that after those witnesses have been cross-examined, the examining magistrate will not believe them and will refuse to commit the accused; perhaps he thinks that those witnesses know more of the particular events than has been related in their written statements; and perhaps he considers he may gain a tactical advantage by causing those witnesses to suffer the ordeal of testifying in court. Whatever his reason, and be it apparently good, bad, or plain stupid to the magistrates and their court clerk, the defence advocate may, if he so wishes, insist on the third – the lengthiest – procedure being followed.

The legislature has required the Magistrates' Court to undertake more and more work, so much so that in order to avoid the courts being overwhelmed, constant attempts are being made to simplify procedures. Unhappily, such simplifications almost always favour the prosecution and encourage the thoughtless and short sighted to "get on with it", so sometimes injustices are done as a result. Justice can never be done in a hurry, and no-one must criticise or be impatient with a defence advocate who does what the law requires him to do – his best for his client, even if he thereby uses the court's valuable time and embarrasses witnesses.

The "paper" committal

An examining magistrate is neither required nor permitted to inquire into the quality of a prosecutor's case during a "paper" committal. The magistrate has merely to ensure that five conditions are satisfied. If those conditions are satisfied, he must commit the accused to stand his trial at the Crown Court; if they are not satisfied, the "paper" committal cannot proceed (and, no doubt, one of the other forms of committal will be arranged on a future date).

The five conditions that must be satisfied are:

(i)   the defendant, or if there is more than one, each defendant is represented by a barrister or solicitor;

(ii) the prosecutor does not call any witness to testify

orally, but tenders written statements in evidence and the defence advocate does not object to this procedure;

(iii) the accused does not himself give evidence orally or call a witness to give evidence orally; but if he wishes the examining magistrate to hear his side of the story (which is unlikely), he is willing to tender his and/or his witness's statements in writing, and the prosecutor does not object to his so doing;

(iv) the defence advocate does not submit or, if there is more than one, none of the defence advocates submits, that the evidence does not disclose a *prima facie* case against his client;

(v) each of the written statements tendered to the examining magistrates complies with the statutory requirements (as set out on page 63).

It is emphasised that during a "paper" committal, an examining magistrate is not concerned with the quality of the evidence, even if the accused tenders his own statement or that of a witness. Such a committal is, essentially, a committal with the consent of both the accused and the prosecutor.

Undoubtedly, a "paper" committal saves much time and labour, and has increasingly been used in appropriate circumstances. Since the procedure may be adopted only when the accused is legally represented, time, labour and money can be saved by granting legal aid to an accused who might perhaps otherwise just miss, for one reason or another, being eligible for it.

Procedure of a "paper" committal

Before the committal starts:

a) the accused or his solicitor must be handed a copy of the written statements that are to be presented to the court;

b) the court must have been informed that the prosecutor intends to follow the "paper" committal procedure.

Nowhere is it laid down how long before the committal date must the defence he handed a copy of each of the statements that will be produced at the committal proceedings. In practice, the prosecutor will present the defence with the requisite copies in time for the defence to study them, otherwise the defence will merely refuse to consent to the simplest form of committal being adopted.

Should one solicitor be representing two or more accused, he must be served with the same number of copies of the written statements as the number of accused for whom he appears.

At the hearing of a "paper" committal, the following steps must be taken:

a) If it has not already been done (as it normally will have been), the charge or charges shall be written down and read to the accused and if the prosecution wish to amend any charges, now is a proper time to do so.

b) The accused and, if there be more than one, each accused shall be asked whether he wishes to:

    (i)   object to any of the prosecution statements being tendered in evidence;

    (ii) give oral evidence himself or call witnesses to testify orally; or

    (iii) submit that the prosecution statements disclose insufficient evidence to put him on trial by jury for the offence or any of the offences with which he is charged.

c) (i)   If the accused answers "yes" to any of those three questions, the proceedings must be halted and all or some, as the case may be, of the prosecutor's witnesses called to testify orally. In practice, the accused will almost certainly be remanded to another date when the required witnesses will attend.

   (ii) If there be more than one accused and one of them agrees to a "paper" committal and the other does not, then the prosecutor must decide whether he can, properly, ask the court to commit the two accused separately. If the accused can, properly, be committed separately, there is no reason why the "paper" committal should not proceed in the case of the one accused but not of the other. In practice, however, the prosecutor will have had a reason why he wanted the accused to be committed together and will still want to have them sent to the higher court (if they are sent at all) together; so an objection to a "paper" committal by one accused will prevent this procedure being followed in the case of the other accused.

d) Should the accused or all the accused answer "no" to each of the three questions in sub-paragraph (b) above, the written statements are handed to the court clerk by the prosecutor.

e) The accused's advocate is then asked whether he wishes to tender written statements by the accused and/or witnesses and if the answer is "yes", the prosecutor is asked if he objects to these statements being handed in. Then:

(i)   if the prosecutor does not object, the statements are tendered and attached to those tendered by the prosecutor; whereas

(ii) if the prosecutor does object, the proceedings are ceased and the same steps taken as would have been taken had an accused not agreed to a "paper" committal.

f) At this stage, the court clerk will probably require a short time in which to check that the tendered statements comply with the laid down requirements (*see* page 63).

g) The examining magistrate then formally commits the accused to stand his trial at the next appropriate Crown Court.

h) Finally, the court may, if it seems appropriate to do so, give the accused the alibi warning and consider applications for bail and a legal aid order by the accused and for costs by the prosecutor (*see* pages 101 and 102).

As was stated earlier, a "paper" committal is a committal by agreement. Almost certainly, the prosecutor and the accused's solicitor will have agreed beforehand that the committal will take this form. If the prosecutor and accused's solicitor have agreed to the procedure, the court may not refuse to follow it; the court's sole responsibility is to ensure that the formalities are correctly dealt with.

The other committal procedures

Occasionally, rather than asking for a purely "paper" committal, an advocate will ask for the statements to be read out. The procedure is basically the same as for a "paper" committal.

Should either the prosecutor or the accused insist or should the accused not be legally represented, one of the other three forms of committals must take place. During each of these committals the examining magistrate has a most important role to play.

At any committal other than a "paper" committal, the accused may not be committed to stand his trial at the Crown Court unless the examining magistrate is satisfied on the evidence adduced before him that the prosecutor has made out a case against the accused. If the examining magistrate decides that the prosecutor has failed to make out a case, the accused is discharged.

Originally, Justices of the Peace discovered and apprehended the criminal and a separate group of people, a Grand Jury, decided whether an accused should stand trial. Later in our history, the justices abandoned their detecting and arresting work to the police and then both a justice and a Grand Jury decided, independently of one another, whether there was sufficient evidence against an accused to warrant his standing trial before a higher court. Today, accused persons have been deprived of the safeguard of the Grand Jury and only an examining magistrate can protect them from oppressive abuses of the court's procedure.

Thus, although the task of an examining magistrate presiding over one of the longer forms of committal is always time-consuming and often boring, it is one of the most important that a justice is required to undertake and never should an examining magistrate be more alert than when an accused's advocate has refused a "paper" committal: the reason he did so may be his knowledge that the prosecutor's case is weak.

Publicity and committals

Should an accused (or one of the accused if there is more than one) ask the examining magistrate for an order authorising the publication and broadcasting of a full report of the committal proceedings, the magistrate must make the order (no matter what the other accused, if there be more than one, may say), otherwise a published or broadcast report of a committal may contain only the following details:

a) the identity of the court and the names of the examining justices;

b) the names, addresses and occupations of the parties and witnesses and the ages of the accused and witnesses;

c) the offence, or offences, or a summary of them, with which the accused person is or persons are charged;

d) the names of the barristers and solicitors engaged in the proceedings;

e) the decision of the court to commit the accused or any of the accused for trial, and any decision of the court on the disposal of the case of any accused not committed;

f) where the court commits the accused or any of the accused for trial, the charge or charges, or a summary of them, on which he is committed and the court to which he is committed;

g) where the committal proceedings are adjourned, the date and place to which they are adjourned;

h) any arrangements as to bail on committal or adjournment; and

i) whether legal aid was granted to the accused or any of the accused.

For this reason, the accused should be told of his right to insist on publicity at the outset of a committal (other, of course, than at a "paper" committal, where there is nothing to report). In fact, an accused is entitled to demand publicity at any stage of the committal and, if that happens, both what was said before, as well as what was said after, the demand may be published and broadcast.

What was said at a committal may be published or broadcast whatever the views of the accused may be:

a) *after* an examining magistrate has decided *not* to commit the accused or (if there is more than one) *all* the accused to stand trial at the Crown Court;

or

b) *after* the trial by the Crown Court of an accused who was, or *all* those accused (if there was more than one) who were, committed to stand trial at the Crown Court.

Public courts

Peculiarly, although the reporting of committals (but not of summary trials) is restricted, a committal must take place in open court, that is, in the presence of any members of the public who wish to attend, unless:

a) there is a specific provision to the contrary in any enactment that is pertinent to the proceedings (for example, the Official Secrets Acts);

b) it appears to the examining magistrate that the ends of justice would not be served by his sitting in public.

The examining magistrate does not have to make an all or nothing decision, since he may, if he thinks it appropriate to do so, exclude the public during part only of the committal and allow it to be present during the rest.

Should an examining magistrate decide to exclude the public during the whole or a part of a committal, reporters must leave with the rest of the public and so, in practice, a magistrate's decision to sit in camera overrides an accused's right to demand that full reporting of the committal be authorised.

Written statements before examining magistrates

Instead of calling a witness to testify orally in court before the examining magistrate, a prosecutor or accused may tender the written statement of the witness so long as the following conditions are complied with:

a) the statement complies with the statutory requirements (*see* page 63);

b) a copy of the statement has been give by the party tendering it to each of the other parties to the proceedings or their legal representatives (and this must be done even if one or more of the accused is not affected by what is in the statement); and

c) none of the other parties objects to the testimony of the witness in question being given in this manner.

A statement for this purpose may be tendered by or on behalf of an accused as well as a prosecutor, although, for the same reasons that an accused rarely testifies at a committal, it is unlikely that the tendering will be done by him.

Unlike a "paper" committal, an accused does not need to be legally represented before a prosecutor or other accused may serve on him a written statement; but the unrepresented accused has the same right as the accused's advocate to insist on the witness giving oral evidence.

No time limit is put on the party tendering a statement by which he must send copies to the other parties. Obviously, he should give the other parties ample time to digest what is written, otherwise at the last minute they may object to the tendering.

Once tendered without objection and accepted by the court, a written statement has the same influence, effect and weight as oral evidence and what is said in it must be weighed and considered by the examining magistrate as carefully and conscientiously as he would oral evidence.

So that an examining magistrate may do this, all the statement (except those parts of it not admissible as evidence) should be read out loud by or on behalf of the party who is tendering it at the stage in the proceedings that he would have called the witness, had the witness been testifying in person.

An examining magistrate may direct that a part of the statement or even the whole of the statement may be précised by the person tendering it rather than reading it in full.

This step should only be taken to avoid unnecessary repetition and never be taken:

a) merely to save time; or

b) if one of the parties asks that the statement be read in full.

Should the examining magistrate consider, at his absolute discretion, that it would be better to have the witness testify orally and be subject to cross-examination, the magistrate may order this of his own volition or at the request of a party to the proceedings and there is nothing to say that the magistrate may not insist on a witness attending, even after the written statement of that witness has been tendered, read and accepted.

Should any part of a written statement be inadmissible as evidence, that part should be marked "treated as inadmissible" and signed by the examining magistrate.

Occasionally, the prosecutor may produce his whole case in the form of written statements, but the committal would not be a "paper" committal.

This could happen, for instance, when a prosecutor originally approached the accused's solicitor and suggested a "paper" committal. The accused's solicitor, perhaps after he had read the statements, might announce that he had no wish to cross-examine the prosecutor's witnesses, nor even, at this stage, to deny the truth of what they said, but that he wished to submit to the examining magistrate that in law or in fact or both the prosecutor had failed to make out a *prima facie* case against the accused. Such an argument is not permitted at a "paper" committal; there one has to:

a) accept the statement; and

b) accept the committal of the accused to the Crown Court without demur or qualification,

or the committal cannot proceed.

No committal, other than a "paper" committal, is a mere formality. At a committal, other than a "paper" committal, the examining magistrate has an important and often difficult part to play and so he must give his complete attention to the tendered statements.

As stated earlier, if the prosecutor or the accused insists, all the witnesses on whom the prosecutor relies to prove his case must attend court and testify orally or, subject to the accused's agreement, the prosecutor may call some witnesses to testify orally and tender the statements of others.

A magistrate's refusal to commit

A refusal by a magistrate (presiding over a committal that is not a "paper" committal) to commit an accused to stand trial does not mean that the accused has been acquitted and may never again be put in peril on that particular charge. A prosecutor who does not agree with the magistrate's refusal to commit may either:

a) re-present the case to another examining magistrate if he has fresh and additional evidence; or

b) apply to a High Court Judge for a Bill of Indictment which, if granted, would result in the accused's being taken before the higher court for trial. This is known as a "Voluntary Bill".

A prosecutor is not necessarily required to produce to the examining magistrate all the evidence on which he will rely at the Crown Court to prove his case against the accused. He need produce only enough evidence for there to be a *prima facie* case against the accused. If he later decides it is necessary for him to adduce evidence additional to that which he called before the examining magistrate, he must provide the accused with a written copy of that evidence before he adduces it at the subsequent trial.

A committal, therefore, serves two important purposes:

a) it ensures that the juries' time is not wasted in trying men who will, patently, be acquitted; and

b) it enables those who are committed for trial to learn what are the prosecutors' cases against them in time for them to prepare their defences.

Committal court procedure when the witnesses testify

The procedure during a committal that is not a "paper" committal is the same as that followed during a summary trial. The prosecutor's witnesses (other than those whose written statements are tendered) are called and subject to:

(i)   examination-in-chief;

(ii) cross-examination; and

(iii) re-examination;

and the same rules of evidence and trial must be obeyed.

As during a summary trial, at the close of the prosecutor's case, the magistrate should insist on there being a momentary pause so that he may mentally review the evidence. The magistrate must check that the prosecutor has proved all that any statute, regulation, or decided case makes it necessary for him to prove. The magistrate must also decide whether a reasonable jury, properly directed by a judge, would be likely to believe the more important of the prosecutor's witnesses.

If the prosecutor has failed to prove one or more of the essential elements of the charge, the magistrate must, without being prompted by the accused's advocate, refuse to commit the accused and release him. This he must do if he considers that a reasonable jury, properly directed, would not believe one or more of the prosecutor's witnesses called with the purpose of proving an essential element.

As during a summary trial (*see* page 58), the accused or his advocate may submit to the examining magistrate that no case has been made out against his client, basing his submission on legal argument, the evidence, or both. The prosecutor may reply only to legal arguments.

If at the close of the prosecutor's case a submission is made that there is "No Case to Answer", the magistrates' decision to commit or not should be made on the basis of whether the evidence is such that a reasonable tribunal might convict.

When the magistrate decides that the accused has a case to answer, he says so publicly, and must warn an unrepresented accused in these words: "You will have an opportunity to give evidence on oath before this court and to call witnesses. But first I am going to ask you whether you wish to say anything in answer to the charge. You need not say anything unless you wish to do so. Anything you say will be taken down and may be given in evidence at your trial. You should take no notice of any promise or threat which any person may have made to persuade you to say anything. Do you wish to say anything in answer to the charge?"

The accused may then give evidence, call witnesses, and be cross-examined by the prosecutor.

An accused, for obvious reasons, seldom discloses his defence at this moment and, if he is wise, confines himself to saying something like, "I have nothing to say at this stage". An unrepresented accused should not be coerced or urged into saying anything that indicates his guilt.

Depositions

During a committal, the testimony of all the witnesses who testify orally is written down by the court clerk, not in question and answer form, but as a continuous statement, called a "deposition". This must be read to and signed by the witness when his evidence is complete. The examining magistrate must also sign it. The accused may obtain copies of the depositions and have them before him when he prepares his defence.

At the subsequent trial, the prosecutor and the judge, but not the jury, are also provided with a copy of the depositions. Thus, because he knows in advance what the evidence will be and will be ready to ensure that the rules of evidence are obeyed, the task of a judge of a higher court is made much simpler than that of a lay magistrate at a summary trial.

The prosecutor is expected to prove the charges on which the accused is before the court; but whether he does so or not, the examining magistrate may have put to the accused, and may commit the accused on, any other charge or charges disclosed during the committal.

A higher court may also prefer other and additional charges, and the higher court may do this no matter what form the committal took.

Rules of evidence and procedure

During a committal that is not a "paper" committal, a few examining magistrates take refuge in the lack of finality in their decision and disregard the rules of evidence and procedure, relying on the higher court to clarify and decide the issues. The fact that information is accepted at the committal does not preclude the higher court from later ruling that it is not evidence. Nevertheless, most examining magistrates are aware of their responsibility to protect the innocent and insist on the many trial rules being observed.

There is, however, a tendency during committals, particularly when the accused is unrepresented, to allow the prosecutor to "get on with it" to the extent, sometimes, of his dictating the witnesses' statements to the court clerk, requiring the witnesses only to say "Yes" periodically.

When an accused is represented and his advocate does not object, this time-saving procedure may be adopted. When the accused is not represented, however, leading questions should be forbidden and never should this rule be more strictly enforced than when a child is testifying. The reason for this is that a magistrate cannot discern a perjuring witness if the witness says no more than "Yes" at infrequent intervals.

No matter how long a court list or busy a magistrate or clerk may be, time is never precious to a magistrate who wishes to do justice and he will insist on the examination-in-chief of witnesses being properly conducted in cases where there is no advocate instructed on behalf of the accused.

The court clerk's task

The court clerk is not required to record the examination of witnesses in question and answer form, only to précis their testimony, so not every reply made by a witness is written into his deposition. When the witness is being cross-examined on behalf of the accused, the wise and courteous clerk does not interrupt the flow of questions directed to a particular issue, but waits until there is a pause or change in the subject of the inquiry to do his writing. Nevertheless, the précis should contain all that the witness said and neither the prosecutor nor the accused may be selective about which answers are recorded.

It may be that many, if not most, committals result in the accused being sent to higher courts for trial and, to that extent, are a mere procedural step. Magistrates should not, however, regard them as such; they are, or should be, an important safeguard to those who have been improperly charged.

Alibi warning

An accused may not adduce evidence in support of an alibi during his trial before one of the higher courts unless:

a) he has given notice that he intends to do so:

    (i) in court during or at the end of the proceedings before the examining magistrate; or

    (ii) to the solicitor for the prosecutor not later than seven days from the end of the committal proceedings; or

b) with the leave of the higher court.

So that an accused may not be taken unaware of this rule, the magistrate (whether presiding over a "paper" or other form of committal), before he announces that he commits the accused to stand trial at a higher court, must ensure that he or the court clerk warns the accused in these words:

"I must warn you that if this court should commit you for trial you may not be permitted at that trial to give evidence of an alibi unless you have earlier given particulars of the alibi and of the witnesses. You may give those particulars now to this court or to the solicitor for the prosecution not later than seven days from the end of these proceedings."

The rules state that the warning need not be given if, having regard to the nature of the offence, it is unnecessary to do so. It is, however, difficult to envisage a set of circumstances wherein it is not feasible, albeit remotely, that an accused might not advance an alibi, as a clutched-at straw. Therefore it is probably sensible to make a habit of always warning an accused. If the oral warning is given, a written warning must also be handed to the accused.

The alibi rule applies only to trials before one of the higher courts. An accused is under no obligation to give a summary court or the prosecutor advance warning of an alibi when he is to be tried summarily.

An application for bail: indictable offence

The question of bail should always be raised and dealt with by an examining magistrate when an accused has been committed for trial.

The procedure to be followed when an application is made is the same as during an earlier remand (*see* page 31).

If bail is refused and the accused is at least eighteen years old and not legally represented, he must be told of his right to apply for bail to a High Court Judge or a Crown Court Judge.

Legal aid

Now is the moment when an accused should ask for legal aid to pay or help to pay for his defence at the higher court.

Opinions differ as to whether there is any duty on the examining magistrate or court clerk to invite an application from an accused who is, in any event, given an explanatory leaflet. Some court clerks avoid enticing an accused to make the request by saying, "Have you any other application?" although such a question is usually incomprehensible to accused persons. On balance it is probably better to be open about the matter and ask the accused whether he wishes to apply for legal aid.

The same rules govern the granting of legal aid for the Crown Court as for a Magistrates' Court.

The prosecutor's costs

At the end of the committal, whether it has been a "paper" committal or not and, if so, whether the accused has been released or committed to stand his trial at a higher court, the barrister or solicitor conducting the prosecution may ask the examining magistrate to award him costs for preparing and presenting to the examining magistrate the prosecution's case. The costs are paid out of Central Funds.

CHAPTER 7

YOUTH COURTS

At one time, a convicted criminal could expect neither sympathy nor understanding from the courts, only retributive punishment. Punishments, being imaginative and sadistic in their cruelty, were disproportionately severe when measured against their offences. Slowly but inevitably, public opinion revolted against these extremes of punishment and it came to be accepted that the age and sex of an offender and the circumstances around the offence should influence the punishment that he or she should suffer.

Later, it was thought proper that juveniles, *i.e.* persons under the age of eighteen years, should generally be treated in a different manner to adults.

Today juveniles, except in a few exceptional circumstances, must be tried in a Youth Court (formerly known as a Juvenile Court).

The court

A Youth Court must, wherever possible, be held in a different building or room from that in which the adult Magistrates' Court sits. If no such other building or room is available, the Youth Court may sit in a room in which sittings of an adult court are held, but only if a sitting of the adult court has not been and will not be held there within an hour before or an hour after the sitting of the Youth Court.

When a special room is available, it is usually designed so that its appearance is not as awe-inspiring as an adult court; for instance, there need be no dock or witness stand and the magistrates sit at a table at floor level or on a very low dais. There is no statutory objection to police officers wearing uniform at a Youth Court, but magistrates should encourage such officers who act as prosecutors and ushers to wear civilian clothing.

A Youth Court is a "closed" court and only members and officers of the court, parties to the case, their legal representatives, witnesses and newspaper reporters may be present. The magistrates may authorise other persons to be present and students and social workers are sometimes permitted to attend. When allowing other persons to be present, magistrates should ensure that the court is not so crowded that the juvenile accused is overawed.

The magistrates

Only magistrates who are "specially qualified" may sit on the panel of a Youth Court. There is no statutory definition of the phrase "specially qualified", except that the maximum age for a member of the Juvenile Panel is 65 and, other than in exceptional circumstances, no one should be elected for the first time to this Bench when he is over 50. They do, however, receive special training. Magistrates are appointed to the Youth Court panel from and by the magistrates for the petty sessional area in which it functions (with the exception of the Inner London area).

The Youth Court magistrate, more than any other, is almost overwhelmed with advice and instruction as to how to deal with accused persons when they are convicted. A Youth Court magistrate, being interested in the welfare of children, is particularly receptive to this advice and instruction. The danger of the emphasis given to this advice and instruction is that the magistrate may overlook the supreme importance of establishing the juvenile's innocence or guilt before the advice and instruction can be put to effective use.

Although magistrates on the Youth Court panel have an onerous task, they are advised to sit regularly and frequently in the adult court, as well as the Youth Court, unless, in the case of Inner London, they have been appointed specifically to the Youth Court. Only by doing so, can a magistrate in the Youth Court ensure that he does not lower his own judicial standard from that which is required of all members of the judiciary.

Who are juveniles?

A juvenile is anyone who has not attained eighteen years.

A child under the age of ten years is considered not capable of committing a criminal act.

A child is a person under the age of fourteen years. Such a person has no right to decline summary trial.

A young person is someone who has attained the age of fourteen but not of eighteen years. Such a person has no right to decline summary trial.

All juveniles must be tried by a jury when charged with homicide and also in the case of certain grave offences where, if found guilty, they would be detained for a long period.

Neither a child nor a young person may be committed to the Crown Court for sentence, although a young person who has attained fifteen years may be committed to the Crown Court if no other method of dealing with him is appropriate, which is very rare indeed and is only where the offence requires it, *e.g.* murder.

A trial in a Youth Court

An accused juvenile is usually made to stand in front of the magistrates with his parents seated behind him while the charges are put to him. If the juvenile denies the accusation, he should be allowed to sit next to his parents or, if he has one, his advocate, so that he may readily seek advice during the trial. There is no purpose in making a juvenile accused stand throughout his trial.

As with an adult, a separate plea of Guilty or Not Guilty must be taken to each charge on which the juvenile is before the court. In the case of a juvenile, however, the plea is taken by asking him whether he admits or denies the charge.

Obviously, as with an adult, the greatest care must be taken to ensure that both the juvenile and his parents understand:

a) the meaning of the charge; and

b) the meaning and possible result of an admission of guilt.

Unless the magistrates are absolutely certain that the juvenile and his parents understand the charge and the purport of an admission of guilt, a plea of Not Guilty must be entered and the onus put on the prosecutor to prove his case.

A denial of guilt by a juvenile

The procedure of the trial of a juvenile who has denied his guilt is the same as that of an adult.

As with an adult, the burden is on the prosecutor to prove the juvenile's guilt beyond all reasonable doubt. The prosecutor must obey the same rules of evidence and procedure as apply during an adult's trial.

So that a juvenile will be as much at his ease as possible and better able to meet the prosecutor's case, the formalities may be relaxed during a juvenile's trial. It is important to note, however, that the relaxation of formality is for the juvenile's benefit and the prosecutor must not be allowed to take advantage of it; any attempt on the part of the prosecutor to do so must be immediately checked.

The rules of evidence and procedure

The rules of evidence and procedure must be obeyed during a juvenile's trial, except that the rules of procedure (but not the rules of evidence) must be relaxed to enable the juvenile to present his case better. This also provides the parents with an opportunity to cross-examine and intervene, if necessary. Despite this relaxation, no information may be introduced in a manner that would not be accepted by an adult court.

Burden of proof

A juvenile, no less than an adult, is innocent until he has been proved guilty beyond all reasonable doubt and, before a child may be convicted, the Bench must be satisfied that he knew at the time that what he did was wrong. Magistrates must not be influenced by a juvenile's appearance or manner during his trial; unless the prosecutor has proved beyond all reasonable doubt that the juvenile is guilty of the particular offence, the juvenile must be acquitted.

Never, never must an accused, whether adult or juvenile, be found guilty merely to uphold anyone's authority, no matter how important that person or his task may be.

A guilty juvenile's history

When it is known that a juvenile is to come before a court, the local Social Services Department is informed, so that the juvenile's past and background may be investigated and reports prepared. Thus, when a juvenile admits committing an offence or is found guilty after a trial, the magistrates have much more information about him than they would about an adult.

Although many officials are required to report on a juvenile, not all of them need to be in court to read their reports to the magistrates and many Local Authorities assign to one official in each department the duty of attending court and reading the reports of all the accused.

A child or young person and his parent or guardian must be sent a copy in advance of any report which the court considers relevant.

Should the magistrates wish to know more of the accused or should the juvenile or his parent, with apparent justification, disagree with the report, the magistrates may remand the accused to another day so that a further report may be prepared, the author of a report attend to be questioned, or evidence refuting the report be called by the accused.

CHAPTER 8

MOTORING OFFENCES

With the possible exception of a dispute between two spouses, no issue is more difficult to decide than one that stems from a motor accident.

Motoring offences are difficult to try because the incidents giving rise to them happen quickly and unexpectedly, so that such witnesses as there are gain only a fleeting and often imperfect impression of those incidents and little reliance can be placed on their assessment of speed and distance. Furthermore, the injured party, with his subsequent civil court claim for compensation in mind, usually wants to pin the blame squarely on the motorist.

The prosecutor

A prosecutor's task and the standard of proof required of him are the same in motoring as in any other criminal charge: if the accused is to be convicted of a motoring offence, the prosecutor must prove his guilt beyond all reasonable doubt.

Seldom is there a legal problem in a charge that arises from a motor accident, the issues usually being purely of fact. For this reason, magistrates are tempted to hear all the evidence, decide who was to blame or primarily to blame and, if that person is the accused, convict him. This is, however, an improper course to adopt.

Never is it more important for a prosecutor to make an opening speech than in a motor accident prosecution. The prosecutor should make clear to the magistrates how the accused's driving was at fault, and unless his evidence satisfactorily proves those faults, the prosecutor has not made out his case against the accused. It is not sufficient for the prosecutor merely to say that the accused drove recklessly or without due care and attention; he must say in what respects the accused's driving was reckless or lacked due care and attention.

Magistrates will bear in mind that the prosecutor has prepared his opening speech by reading the statements of his witnesses and if, when giving evidence, those witnesses fail to substantiate what the prosecutor said in his speech, the magistrates should be most suspicious of them.

Magistrates are, again, advised to ignore the fact that a participant in the accident was injured, whether severely or not. One motorist may drive with flagrant recklessness and not do damage or cause injury, while another may be involved in, yet wholly blameless for, an accident in which a man is killed.

The need for a plan

It is not easy to give a verbal picture of a road, and witnesses frequently become incoherent when attempting verbally to describe the scene of an accident.

Few civil and higher criminal courts will accept rough and inaccurate plans, yet prosecutors regularly ask magistrates to base their decisions on such plans.

Furthermore, although the plans are acknowledged to be distorted, witnesses are asked to indicate on them the positions of various objects and people. It is not, therefore, surprising that the resultant mental pictures of accidents are as distorted as the plans on which they are based.

If a plan is necessary, and in most motor accident cases one is, the magistrates should, as do professional judges, insist on being provided with a *scale* plan, on which are marked pillar boxes, road signs, lamp posts, etc. It is simpler and conveys a more accurate impression for a witness, after looking at an accurate plan, to say, "I was standing by the pillar box when the car was by the third lamp post," than for him to guess the various distances.

Should no scaled plan be available, magistrates are advised not to use an inaccurate diagram, but rather to rely on the verbal descriptions of the witnesses.

Magistrates with local knowledge

There are occasions when a magistrate has personal knowledge of the locality of an accident. Such a magistrate is permitted to rely on that knowledge, but it is rarely wise for him to do so when trying the subsequent case because:

a) his memory may not be accurate;

b) his mental picture may not coincide with that of a colleague and the witnesses; and

c) he cannot be cross-examined so that the quality of his memory may be gauged.

Were a magistrate to rely on his memory and also wish to be fair to the prosecutor and the accused, he would have to describe to them the memory picture he has of the locality. In all probability, there would be disagreement as to the accuracy of this memory picture, and the magistrate would be in a most embarrassing position.

The Highway Code

Magistrates are reminded that the Highway Code has not the same force as an Act of Parliament or a regulation: indeed, the Act of Parliament that authorises its publication states specifically that failure to observe any provision of the Code does not, of itself, render a person liable to criminal proceedings. But, of course, a failure to observe the Highway Code may be relied on by either party to the proceedings as tending to establish or negative any liability which is in question.

Thus, the mere fact that a motorist has not exactly obeyed the, in some cases rather vague, advice set out in the Highway Code should not, alone, cause him to be convicted.

The close of the prosecutor's case

As during any trial, at the close of the prosecutor's case, the magistrates require a moment's thought in which to decide whether the prosecutor has proved all that, in law, he is required to prove before a conviction can be sustained; and if the prosecutor has failed to do so, the accused must, of course, be acquitted.

Additionally, however, the magistrates must ask themselves, "Are we clear in what manner the prosecutor alleges that the accused drove without due care and attention?" If the magistrates are not clear in what respect the accused is alleged to have done wrong, or are not satisfied that the accused has misbehaved in the manner alleged by the prosecutor, the accused must be acquitted without being called upon to put his defence to the Bench.

The sentence

Patently, motorists who misbehave should be punished, yet the punishment must fit not only the crime, but the criminal.

When fining a motorist, the magistrates should take into consideration all the factors to be borne in mind when imposing any financial penalty. In motorist cases, however, magistrates should also be influenced by the motorist's occupation: a weekend motorist may be a selfish and incompetent driver yet have driven for twenty years (although only on Saturdays and Sundays) without committing an offence, whereas a lorry driver or travelling sales representative may build up a record of minor convictions in a comparatively short period merely because he is on the road day after day. On the other hand, a bad driver who is on the roads only at weekends has less opportunity to do damage than the bad driver who is behind the wheel day in and day out.

Magistrates must always discriminate between individuals when passing sentence, but never more so than when dealing with motorists. Unhappily, many Benches have set penalties for various classes of motoring offences. After all, few motorists intend to have accidents yet, of all offenders, they are the most heavily punished for doing what they did not intend to do.

Finally, magistrates should not increase the sentence merely because someone was injured or harmed in the accident giving rise to the charge: magistrates are reminded that it is the accused's misbehaviour that warrants punishment and, in a motor accident, the damage done is often not commensurate with the extent of the misbehaviour.

Many motoring offences carry obligatory endorsement of the driver's licence and attract varying amounts of penalty points. The magistrate would be wise to seek the advice of the clerk as to this aspect of the proceedings, although as a magistrate gains experience he may well become familiar with many of these cases. The same applies to disqualification from driving where some offences carry obligatory, and others discretionary, disqualifications.

Totting up and penalty points

Where a motorist is convicted of an endorsable offence and in the three years prior to the date of the commission of this offence his licence was endorsed and the penalty points already on his licence plus the penalty points awarded in the current proceedings amount to or exceed twelve points, magistrates must disqualify the motorist, unless it is proved to their satisfaction that to do so would result in exceptional hardship to the motorist, in which case they have a discretion not to disqualify.

This discretion may be exercised in favour of a convicted motorist once only in a three year period. This is a very tricky area for magistrates and they would be wise to rely on the advice and guidance given by their clerk.

CHAPTER 9

LEGAL AID IN CRIMINAL MATTERS

Legal aid is available to those individuals who qualify for it whether they are involved in a civil or criminal trial. Legal aid is, however, available only to actual persons: artificial, albeit legally recognised, entities such as limited companies are not entitled to legal aid.

Magistrates may grant legal aid to:

a) a person who is charged with a criminal offence and is to be dealt with in the Magistrates' Court;

b) a person who is appealing to the Crown Court against his conviction or sentencing by a Magistrates' Court (although this is normally dealt with by the Crown Court);

c) the respondent to an appeal to the Crown Court;

d) an accused for the purpose of the committal proceedings;

e) a person who has been committed to stand his trial at the Crown Court; and

f) a person who, having been convicted by the magistrates, is committed to the Crown Court for sentence.

Applications for legal aid to appeal from a decision of the magistrates on a point of law, by way of case stated to a divisional court are made to the appropriate Legal Aid Board office and not the Magistrates' Court.

Barrister and solicitor

The granting of legal aid for an appearance in the Magistrates' Court normally entitles the applicant to the services of a solicitor only. When the case is unusually grave or difficult, however, magistrates may assign a barrister as well as a solicitor.

In practice, by assigning a barrister, the magistrates are increasing the fees payable to the lawyers. Even when the magistrates do not assign a barrister, a solicitor may brief a barrister to appear in court; but if he does so, he must share with the barrister the money he would have been paid had he appeared himself.

The mere fact that more money is paid to the lawyers is not, however, a reason why a barrister should not be assigned in unusually grave or difficult cases; such cases cause the lawyers additional work and responsibility, and there is no reason why they should not be recompensed accordingly.

The granting of legal aid in proceedings at the Crown Court automatically permits the solicitor to brief one barrister. When the case involves a murder charge, magistrates have the power to assign two barristers, which probably means that one will be a Queen's Counsel and the other a junior (that is, an ordinary barrister such as normally appears in the Magistrates' Courts) who will appear for the applicant at his trial.

Magistrates' power to delegate the consideration of legal aid applications

Magistrates are permitted to refer applications for legal aid to their clerk. Probably, most magistrates, in order to save their own time, will delegate their responsibility for considering applications to their clerk.

A clerk has not, however, the same authority as have his magistrates. A clerk may:

a) grant an application;

b) in appropriate circumstances, refuse an application unless the applicant makes a financial contribution (*see* page 116); or

c) refer the application to one of his magistrates or a full Bench.

A clerk has no authority to refuse an application. Only a magistrate or Bench of magistrates may refuse an application. Thus, when a clerk does not feel that he should grant an application, he must refer to it to a magistrate or Bench. If it is further refused, the applicant may appeal to the Legal Aid Board office.

Written statement of means

An applicant must furnish a written statement of his means on the prescribed form before his application may be considered. So long as he has handed the statement of means to the court (in practice, usually to the office of the justices' clerk), an applicant may make an oral application to the Bench for legal aid at one of his appearances in court. On the other hand, he may make his application in writing (again on a prescribed form) and hand the application in with his statement of means.

Oral and written applications

An accused has the right to apply for legal aid, and may do so in writing or orally. Obviously, time is saved if applications are made in writing; but, since he has the right to apply orally in court, a Bench may not properly be impatient with or critical of an applicant who makes an oral application. After all, he is merely exercising a legal right, and may have an excellent reason for doing so.

When legal aid should be granted

Legal aid should be granted when:

a) an applicant cannot afford to pay any or all of the cost of his being represented by a lawyer; and

b) it is desirable in the interests of justice that the accused should have legal aid.

However, where there is more than one accused, if there is no conflict of interest between them, the court should assign one solicitor.

The applicant's financial need for legal aid

An applicant for legal aid may be considered to:

a) have sufficient financial resources to pay all his legal costs;

b) have sufficient financial resources to contribute at least something towards his legal costs; or

c) be so poor that it would not be reasonable to expect him even to contribute towards his legal costs.

An applicant within the first group must be refused legal aid, no matter what other merit his application may have.

In the case of applicants falling within the second and third groups, the second ground – the interests of justice – for granting their applications must be considered. If the application is granted:

a) an applicant within the second group will, in due course, be required to make an appropriate contribution towards his legal costs; and

b) an applicant within the third group will be given free legal aid.

The applicant's means

Regulations set out the manner in which an applicant's means for the purpose of legal aid must be calculated. The regulations and the calculations are complicated. Magistrates are, of course, entitled to do the calculations themselves if they so wish, and should do so if an applicant alleges that the regulations have not been complied with when his means were calculated. Normally, however, a magistrate will rely on his clerk to do the necessary calculations.

An applicant's contribution

Peculiarly, an applicant who has been granted legal aid but is required to contribute towards his legal costs, does not start to pay his contribution immediately the grant of legal aid is made (unless, of course, he is required to make a down payment). Only at the conclusion of the proceedings may the magistrates order the applicant to pay the requisite contribution, if appropriate, by instalments.

The regulations set out the manner in which the maximum contribution that an applicant may be ordered to pay is to be calculated.

It is important to remember that an applicant who is liable to be ordered to pay a contribution may be ordered to make the payment even if he is acquitted.

A down payment

Should the applicant be likely to be liable to make a contribution at the end of the proceedings and/or if he has the means to make an immediate payment, the magistrates may order that legal aid should be refused unless a down payment on account of costs is made.

Legal aid generally

As was stated in the introduction to this book, the real value of our lay magistracy is that it reflects public opinion – and it is of value only so long as it does so.

Individual magistrates may criticise the granting of legal aid as being a waste of public money. They may be right; but just as the public have come to expect medical care from the National Health Service, and legal aid to bring or defend civil claims, so too is it aware of the need for legal aid in criminal matters. Parliament has recognised the need; so must the magistracy.

Once, no one who was granted legal aid was required to pay anything towards the legal costs; legal aid was either refused or it was free and, as a result, foolish decisions were made. Some magistrates, for instance, appeared to assume that everyone specially saved twenty or thirty pounds in readiness for when he was accused of a crime. That assumption need no longer be made; the applicant who can afford to contribute towards the legal costs can be made to do so.

Finally, a word for the motorist. To a travelling sales representative, the man who lives far from his place of work, a goods vehicle driver, a housewife with children or a sick parent, a policeman on motor patrol, a television repairman, and so on, a driving licence is as important as a solicitor's annual practising certificate – yet many magistrates are reluctant to grant those accused of motoring offences a legal aid order. Driving without due care and attention, or at a speed in excess of a speed limit is as much a crime as is stealing or indecently exposing one's person – and the consequences of a conviction for it may be infinitely more disastrous to the accused and his family, so why should the man or woman accused of a motoring crime not have the benefit of legal aid?

Legal aid should not be granted or refused willy-nilly. No

matter what the alleged crime may be, each and every applicant for legal aid is entitled to have his application carefully, individually, and humanely considered.

CHAPTER 10

CIVIL JURISDICTION

The jurisdiction of magistrates to try civil cases is strictly limited, and in every case depends upon there being an Act of Parliament that specifically grants such judicial powers.

The two civil issues with which magistrates are most frequently concerned are domestic proceedings and those affecting the welfare of children.

Each year many thousands of marriages break down for one reason or another, but the parties do not necessarily want a divorce. It may be that divorce is repugnant on account of religious beliefs or that the parties have not been married for the one year period that is usually necessary for divorce, or that one of the spouses does not wish the other to have his or her "freedom".

In such cases, where the spouses live apart but are not divorced, it is thought proper that the better-off spouse who can afford to do so should contribute towards the maintenance of the other spouse. The latter may, without asking for a divorce, apply to the County Court which deals with divorces for maintenance but such an application can take a long time and be expensive, so the task of trying those cases where more immediate relief is sought has been given to the magistrates.

Magistrates will also hear applications for the custody of and access to the children of the marriage, and for orders for the protection of a spouse or child of the family from the violence or threatened violence of the other spouse.

Matrimonial proceedings may be heard only by specially constituted domestic courts consisting of magistrates appointed to a special panel.

Grounds for a maintenance order
Until fairly recently the grounds on which spouses might ask for maintenance in the Magistrates' Court were not the same as those on which they may petition for a divorce, but the law

has now been changed to bring Magistrates' Courts into line with the Divorce Courts.

In general terms, the magistrates may make an order for maintenance to a person whose spouse has:

a) failed to provide reasonable maintenance for that spouse;

b) failed to provide or make a proper contribution towards reasonable maintenance for any child of the family; (A child of the family is such if it is treated, not merely accepted, as such.)

c) behaved in such a way that the other spouse could not reasonably be expected to live with him or her;

d) deserted him or her for any length of time.

Who may be a complainant

It is important to note that either a wife or a husband may make application to a Magistrates' Court.

Powers of the magistrates

The magistrates have wide powers when an application is made to them, but are usually only called on to decide:

a) what maintenance should be paid;

b) who should have custody of any child of the family who is under eighteen;

c) as to access to (or, more accurately, contact with) a child by a parent with whom the child will not be residing;

d) as to the giving of protection to one spouse against the other;

e) whether to order a lump sum payment.

Conciliation procedure

After an application has been issued, it is the normal practice for the clerk to hold a preliminary hearing in private in one of his offices – as opposed to a court room – to which all parties and/or their legal representatives are invited, to ascertain precisely what issues are at stake and to see what matters, if any, can possibly be agreed prior to the first court hearing.

The clerk may give, vary or revoke directions for the conduct of the proceedings, *e.g.* the timetable, service of documents, etc.

The magistrate's difficulties

(a) Unscrupulous parties

A troublesome feature of a dispute between spouses is that most parties are prepared to be ruthless and unscrupulous in order to "win" the case; and since most family members are intensely partisan, a Bench seldom has an impartial witness on whom it can rely.

(b) Lack of prior information

A second difficulty is the lack of prior information about the allegations to be made and the issues involved as the Bench, and sometimes even the defendant, has no more than the bald statement on the summons containing the allegation.

The effect of a verdict

Despite the difficulties and the unpleasant behaviour of the parties, magistrates must remember that their decision will almost certainly have a profound effect on the future of the parties and their children. Magistrates must also remember that the burden of proof is on the party making an allegation, and unless that burden is discharged by the calling of proper evidence the summons must be dismissed.

Magistrates must not be affected by religious bias or inherent prejudices, nor must they give a decision because they think that decision is "best for the family". No matter how bad for the family or otherwise harsh it may be, the magistrates' decision must be based on and follow the evidence.

The advocates

At one time the majority of complainants and defendants were not represented by lawyers, but the scope of the Legal Aid and Advice Act has been extended to include domestic disputes. Applications for legal aid are made by the parties to a local Legal Aid Board office and magistrates should be sympathetic to a complainant or defendant who asks for an adjournment because there has been no time for his application for legal aid to be considered.

The duty of an advocate appearing for a complainant or a defendant is the same as that of an advocate representing an accused during a criminal trial.

Reconciliation

Almost always, a dispute between a husband and wife has tragic results for the spouses and their children. Magistrates are therefore tempted to try to bring about a reconciliation.

Advocates are under a duty to ensure that, if there is a distinct possibility that a reconciliation may be effected, all facilities should be granted to the parties. However, a lawyer owes a duty to a client who is contemplating a reconciliation with his or her spouse to point out the consequences of such reconciliation. If a lawyer omitted to point out the fact, he would be failing in his duty, and might be sued for negligence.

A magistrate's role is that of impartial judge and not of peacemaker. Furthermore, he is not sitting in a court of morals, where the verdict goes to the morally right. A domestic court is a court of law, and its verdict must go to the party who is legally entitled to it. Therefore a magistrate must not allow his decision to be influenced by a refusal to be reconciled.

Burden of proof

Matrimonial disputes must be tried with the same disinterested impartiality as any other judicial enquiry. In criminal proceedings, a very high standard of proof is demanded of a prosecutor; before the magistrates may convict the prosecutor must prove the accused's guilt beyond all reasonable doubt. Similarly, in civil cases, the magistrates may find in a complainant's favour only if they decide that, on the balance of probabilities, the allegations are true. The burden of proof in a matrimonial dispute is squarely on the complainant, be that person a husband or a wife, and the complainant must prove the allegations which he or she makes to the required standard if the Bench is to find the case proved. However, the actual standard demanded of complainants attempting to prove the various grounds may be changed from time to time by the decisions of higher courts and the wise magistrate will therefore ask his court clerk what is the current standard at the outset of any matrimonial dispute.

No matter how sorry for a complainant a magistrate may be, and even if in his heart he believes that the complainant has been maltreated, the charge against the defendant must be dismissed unless the complainant has proved to the required standard of satisfaction by properly introduced evidence each and every necessary ingredient of the charge.

Although there is no rule of law that says he must, the wise and judicially minded magistrate to whom information is improperly related will adjourn the case to be heard by a fresh Bench.

Procedure of a domestic or Family Proceedings court

The order in which witnesses are called and the manner in which they may be questioned are the same during domestic proceedings as during the summary trial of a criminal charge.

As during a summary criminal trial, the complainant or his (or her) advocate may make an opening speech during which he relates the facts that he anticipates he will prove, and if he mentions the applicable law he must tell the Bench of *all* the law (whether in his client's favour or not) that is pertinent to the issues.

Before calling his evidence, the defendant or his (or her) advocate may, if he wishes, make an opening speech. Should he decide to do so, the following three rules apply:

   (i)   he may not make a second speech at the close of all the evidence unless he has called to the witness box the defendant and at least one other witness;

   (ii) even then, he may make the second speech only if the Bench gives him permission to do so (and the permission is usually given); and

   (iii) if the defendant or his (or her) advocate makes that second speech, the complainant or his (or her) advocate is entitled, as of right, to make the closing speech.

Thus, unlike during the summary trial of a criminal offence, by making two speeches the defendant or his advocate will lose the right to make the final speech.

Submission of "No Case to Answer"

At the close of the applicant's case, it is important that the magistrates should have a moment's pause in which to consider what they have heard. The need for this pause is particularly important because of an established practice peculiar to the Family Division of the High Court. When at the close of the complainant's case:

a) a submission is made on behalf of the defendant that no case has been made out against him; and

b) the Bench rules that there is a case for him to answer,

then neither the defendant nor a witness on his behalf is permitted to give evidence.

This practice must be followed by the magistrates only when trying a domestic matter.

The reason for the practice is not easily understood, and it throws a heavy – many think an unfair and unreasonable – burden on the defendant's advocate: should he think there is no case against his client, he dare not risk the submission in case it is overriden and his client may not "have his say", yet by calling his client he may supply the omissions in the complainant's case.

So drastic to the defendant in domestic proceedings are the consequences of an unsuccessful submission of "No Case to Answer" that many court clerks warn advocates, and particularly inexperienced ones, of these consequences before the advocates embark on this submission.

Magistrates must therefore pay careful heed to any submission that there is not case for the defendant to answer, because it will not have been made lightly.

However, it should be stressed that since recent changes in legislation, the chances of this situation now arising in a domestic court are lessening.

The end of the complainant's case

Whether or not a submission of "No Case to Answer" has been made, and whether or not the defendant is legally represented, at its close a magistrate should consider the complainant's case. He should ask himself in respect of each complaint against the defendant:

a) what must the complainant prove before I may find in his or her favour? and

b) has the complainant proved these essentials to my proper judicial satisfaction?

Then :

(i) where the answer to the second question is "No", the case must immediately be dismissed;

(ii) when a submission of "No Case to Answer" has been made, the chairman must announce that the Bench finds "proved" those allegations in respect of which the answer to the second question was "Yes";

(iii) when there has been no submission of "No Case to Answer", the mere fact that the answer to the second question was "Yes" does not mean that the complainant's case has been proved: the burden of proof remains on the complainant until the close of *all* the evidence.

The magistrates' verdict

Only when all the evidence has been called by both sides and the final speech made may the magistrates decide whether the complainant's case has been proved. That decision must be based on nothing other than properly related evidence.

Custody of children

Magistrates are often required to decide with which parent a child under eighteen years should live and how much the other parent should contribute towards the child's upkeep.

Magistrates have a wide discretion when making a custody order (now formally known as a "residence order"), and may make an order in respect of a child when none is made in respect of a parent. For instance, a wife may desert her husband and so not be entitled to maintenance from him, yet the magistrates may give her custody of a child of the marriage and order the husband to pay maintenance in respect of that child.

No matter where the legal and moral blame may be, when spouses quarrel their children – who are usually blameless – are the principal sufferers and their misery is often increased by one parent using them as a weapon against the other.

Before making a residence and maintenance order, the magistrates must listen carefully to what is said by or on behalf of each parent, but in the end they must treat the children's interests as being of paramount importance.

When deciding with which parent a child should live, magistrates will take into consideration the emotional, affectionate, physical and financial background that each parent can offer. All things being equal, however, the following principles usually apply:

a) a young child should seldom be taken from its mother unless the mother is proved to be physically or morally incapable of caring for it;

b) a mother who is living in "respectable" adultery with one man should not be deprived of her children for that reason alone;

c) the preferences of older children as to with which parent they want to live should be given great weight.

If asked to do so by the parent who has been deprived of the custody of the child, the magistrates should make an order granting reasonable contact with that parent. In certain cases, magistrates are asked to specifically define the terms of the contact granted. For instance, if the mother and father cannot agree on the terms of contact, the magistrates may deal with this aspect of the proceedings as a completely separate issue. The magistrates will be asked to determine the frequency with which contact may take place and subject to what conditions.

To assist them in making this very difficult decision, the magistrates may have ordered the Court Welfare Office (i.e. a probation officer) to interview all interested parties and to prepare a report. This Welfare Report will be read at the conclusion of the evidence but its contents are only recommendations and the opinion of a qualified and independent observer and are not binding on magistrates.

Assessment of maintenance

Matrimonial proceedings are not brought to punish an erring spouse, but merely to make him (or her) meet his proper financial obligations to his family. A maintenance order *must not*, therefore, be a punitive one, but must be based on the incomes, responsibilities and proper expenditures of the two spouses. When considering the surrounding circumstances, magistrates must remember that what is an essential expenditure in one walk of life is a luxury in another, and must view the problem with the outlook of the husband and wife in question.

Orders for payment of lump sums

Magistrates may also make an order requiring payment of a lump sum, either in addition to, or in place of, periodical payments.

There is a maximum limit to the amount of any lump sum so ordered to be paid but no restriction on the number of times orders for lump sums may be made, with power to order a further lump sum payment when a maintenance order is varied.

Giving protection

Magistrates may be asked for an order protecting one spouse from the violence, either actual or threatened, of the other.

They may grant a personal protection order which prevents the other spouse from using or threatening to use violence against the other and/or a child of the family.

They may make an exclusion order compelling the other spouse to quit the matrimonial home or be barred from entering it.

An exclusion order can be made where violence has been used against the complainant or a child of the family, or threats of violence have been made against either and there is evidence available of violence to another person or if a personal protection order has been broken by the threat or use of violence.

Magistrates may also order one spouse to allow the other to enter and remain in the matrimonial home.

Proceedings relating to paternity

The purpose of a paternity order is not the punishment of the father, but to ensure that he contributes towards the maintenance of his child. Peculiarly, the right to bring the proceedings is personal to the child's mother (and, in certain circumstances, the Department of Social Security or Local Authority) and should she die before bringing them, none other may do so in her place. But once the order has been made it may be varied so that the payment is made to whoever is actually caring for the child.

The child's mother must be a "single" woman before she may bring proceedings. Obviously an unmarried woman is a single woman, as is a divorcee and a widow, but a married woman is also a "single" woman for these purposes if she can satisfy the Bench that, at the date of the birth of her child, she was living apart from her husband and had lost the right to be maintained by him.

Application for a paternity summons

The mother may apply to the court for a summons against the alleged father:

a) before the birth;

b) at any time within three years of the birth; or

c) if the alleged father has ceased to reside in England before the birth or within three years after the birth, within twelve months after the alleged father's return to England.

Once the above three periods have expired, the mother may not apply for a summons unless:

a) within three years after the child's birth the alleged father paid money for the child's maintenance; or

b) the mother proves that before the child's birth she was party to a marriage to the alleged father which was invalid by reason of either party's being under-age, and the alleged father had access to her within the twelve months before the child's birth.

If either of these two events occurred, the mother may make an application at any time.

Burden of proof

Magistrates must try such a dispute with the same disinterested impartiality as any other judicial enquiry.

The burden of proof is squarely on the mother to prove that the defendant is the father of the child which is the subject of the proceedings. The same high standards of proof are not demanded as in the case of criminal proceedings and the magistrates may find in the complainant's favour if they only decide that on the balance of probabilities what she alleges is true.

The order

There is no maximum amount that the putative father may be ordered to pay in respect of each child: this will depend upon the surrounding circumstances but it is important to remember that the defendant is required to contribute to the maintenance of his child only, and not to the maintenance of the child and its mother.

Unless there is a good reason to do otherwise, magistrates should order the defendant to pay the maintenance to their justices' clerk.

Magistrates may also make an order providing for the payment of a lump sum to enable liabilities or expenses reasonably incurred before the making of the order to be met, *e.g.* in respect of birth expenses or in maintaining the child. The court clerk will advise as to the maximum lump sum payment that can be ordered.

Under certain circumstances, the Department of Social Security or a Local Authority may apply for a summons.

Other civil proceedings

In addition to domestic or family proceedings, magistrates

have jurisdiction to hear a number of other civil issues where they have been specifically granted powers by Act of Parliament.

These include, the recovery of money by way of civil debt, *e.g.* Council Tax; applications for consent to marriage by those under-age; personal applications for a noise abatement order; the stopping up and diversion of highways by local authorities; and appeals and applications for determination in respect of local authority requirements under the Public Health Acts and similar legislation.

Proceedings relating to children

Before 1991, proceedings relating to the welfare of children were heard in the Juvenile Court but the Family Proceedings Court has now taken over such matters. The jurisdiction of this family court now encompasses all the old child care law but with new powers to make a whole variety of orders such as a contact, prohibited steps, residence or specific issue order.

It should be borne in mind by magistrates sitting on this Bench that the primary concern of the court is the welfare of the child and that the purpose of the most recent legislation, the Children Act 1989, is to provide a clear and comprehensive framework of powers and responsibilities which will hopefully secure the anticipated goal of Parliament that children receive the care, upbringing and protection they deserve.

Magistrates sitting in the Family Proceedings Court are therefore likely to hear applications by mothers, fathers (both married or unmarried to each other), grandparents, school attendance officers, Local Authority solicitors and social workers, and will have available before them a whole variety of powers and orders. These include Emergency Protection and Child Assessment Orders which deal with immediate serious situations where there is deep concern for the welfare of a child, orders for residence and contact and, under certain circumstances, full adoption orders.

For further information relating to the Family Proceedings Court, see *"Family Proceedings – the Magistrates' Guide"* by John Greenhill, published by Shaw & Sons (ISBN 0 7219 1350 4).

CHAPTER 11

EVIDENCE GENERALLY

The fundamental principle

It is a fundamental principle of justice that:

a) people must be judged only on information that is acceptable as evidence; and

b) evidence must be produced to a court in accordance with certain rules.

If this fundamental principle is forgotten or disregarded during a criminal or civil trial, justice is being denied to one or both of the parties; and if during a criminal trial, it is almost always the prosecutor who gains an advantage.

Magistrates are not expected to know by heart the rules of evidence and, therefore, must listen carefully when either advocate or the court clerk voices an objection to some piece of information being given as evidence or to the manner in which the evidence is being extracted from a witness. Although there is no rule of law that they must, wise magistrates, when they realise that they have been told something of importance that is not evidence or have been told it in an improper manner (by means, for instance, of a leading question), halt the trial and adjourn it for a rehearing by another Bench. Furthermore, when magistrates are in doubt whether or not to adjourn a case, they would be wise to resolve the doubt by an adjournment.

The admission or exclusion of a piece of information as evidence may be the basis of an appeal and, therefore, many court clerks carefully record any objection that an advocate may make as to the introduction or mode of introduction of information and the magistrates' decision.

Protection of those accused of crimes

The British have long held the view that it is preferable for many guilty men to be acquitted than for one innocent man to be wrongly convicted, and from this belief stems most of our rules of evidence in and procedure for criminal trials. Indeed, it is now generally recognised that, although the rules of evidence must be strictly applied to prosecutors and parties to civil disputes, a man who is being prosecuted for a criminal charge should be allowed a measure of latitude.

Burden of proof

In this country a Bench is not given a right of roving inquiry to unearth the truth during either a criminal or civil trial. We prefer the "accusatory" process, whereby a prosecutor or complainant:

a) accuses a named individual;

b) of being guilty of a specified legal wrong.

During the trial the one party attempts to prove his accusation or case, while the other party endeavours to disprove or cast doubt on it. The parties, their advocates, and the Bench are interested only in the accusation; and if members of the Bench neither believe the witnesses who support it nor accept the legal arguments on which it is based, the prosecutor or complainant has failed in his purpose no matter what other sins or omissions on the part of the accused person may have come to light during the trial.

The general burden of proving his or her case remains on the prosecutor or complainant throughout the trial and it is not for the accused or defendant to prove his or her innocence.

Burden of proof in criminal trials

Except in the case of a few offences, the burden of proof is on a prosecutor to prove the accused's guilt, and not on the accused to prove his innocence.

Normally, the burden remains on the prosecutor throughout the trial. For instance, the fact that an accused sets up an alibi as a defence does not transfer the burden of proving the alibi to be true beyond all reasonable doubt on to him; and if, at the end of the trial, the magistrates have sensible doubts as to the truth of the alibi, they must give the benefit of the doubt to the accused and dismiss the case.

The weight or burden of proof does not vary from crime to crime; a prosecutor is required to prove an accused's guilt beyond all reasonable doubt.

Burden of proof on an accused

The offences and occasions when the burden of proof is transferred from the prosecutor to the accused are so few and rare that magistrates should assume that the burden is on the prosecutor, unless told by their court clerk to the contrary.

When the burden is put on an accused to prove his innocence, the standard of proof required of him is nothing like as high as that demanded of a prosecutor; an accused who is required to prove his innocence need do no more than prove that his defence could reasonably be true.

Relevance

Evidence is information that tends or helps to prove or disprove the issue before the court, and information that does not do so must be excluded.

For the magistrates to be told that a pedestrian was maimed in an accident does not help them judge a motorist's driving behaviour; that there is a wave of shop-lifting does not prove the dishonesty of a particular person; and an accused's discourtesy when arrested proves nothing more than that he is discourteous. Yet prosecutors frequently introduce information similar to these examples which in no way helps to prove the alleged commission of the offence, but may well have a prejudicial effect on the Bench.

Magistrates should be on their guard against being influenced by irrelevant information and should rebuke any advocate who introduces it.

There are a few, rarely occurring, circumstances when apparently irrelevant information may be properly introduced, and the court clerk will advise the Bench of these occurrences. Then, the magistrates must insist on its being explained to them:

　　a) the purpose for which the information is admitted as evidence; and

b) how much value they may put on the information if they accept it as true.

Leading questions

A leading question is one which:

a) is so phrased as to suggest the answer required; and

b) is asked about something that is in issue between the parties to the dispute.

An advocate *must not* ask leading questions of witnesses whom he has called to the witness box, during his examination-in-chief and re-examination.

An advocate *may* ask leading questions during his cross-examination.

This rule is misunderstood or deliberately flouted by many advocates, and magistrates can cause advocates to obey this and other such rules by halting any trials in which they have improperly received information as a result of leading questions, and sending the case to another Bench.

Witnesses' notes and policemen's note books

Normally a witness must give his evidence without reference to any written memorandum or statement.

A witness may refer to a note in order to refresh his memory about the incident on which his testimony is based, but only if:

a) the witness has some memory (without reference to his notes) of the incident; and

b) the note was made at the time of, or shortly after, the occurrence of the incident.

A witness may merely refresh his memory from his notes, and may not read the notes verbatim. Should his memory of the incident wholly fail him, he may not substitute the notes for his memory.

Once a witness has referred to his notes, the opposing advocate may read them.

A police officer's note is no more privileged than that of any other witness.

Hearsay evidence

Generally, a witness may tell the magistrates only of what he saw with his own eyes or heard with his own ears and may not repeat what he was told by a third party.

There are exceptions to this important rule but, unless authoritatively advised to do otherwise by their court clerk, magistrates should exclude all "second-hand" evidence.

When magistrates are advised to listen to hearsay evidence, they must inquire the purpose of their being told it, since the reasons for admitting such evidence are not always the same.

Two of the exceptions occur with sufficient frequency to warrant special mention; they are:

1. Normally, Smith may not relate to the court what Smith told Brown or what Brown told Smith. If, however, the conversation took place in the hearing of the accused, the accused's reaction to what was said is important. If the accused's reaction was that of an innocent man, that fact must count in his favour. If it was that of a guilty man, that fact should count against him. If, however, the accused did not react, or his reaction cannot be proved, the Smith and Brown conversation has no evidential value.

   Therefore, before evidence of the conversation is related, the chairman or (more probably) the court clerk should ask the prosecutor whether the accused reacted when he heard what was said, and if the answer is that the accused did not react, the court should not be told of the conversation.

2. Recent complaints made by a woman or child that she or he has been the victim of a sexual offence is admissible as evidence in certain circumstances.

   The purpose of admitting this evidence is:

   a) to rebut or confirm an allegation of consent in a charge to which consent would be a defence; and

   b) as a protection to the accused to indicate whether or not the alleged victim's behaviour was consistent with that of someone who had been sexually assaulted.

A recent complaint must never be treated as in any way proving the facts alleged by the prosecutor: it is at best a yardstick by which the prosecutor's other evidence is measured. If the complaint and other evidence differ materially, magistrates should be suspicious of the prosecutor's case.

General matters

Magistrates must not:

a) allow a witness to be treated as hostile;

b) require one spouse to give evidence against the other if they are unwilling so to do;

c) allow reference to be made to an accused person's character or previous convictions unless they have already been introduced by the defence;

d) after an objection by his advocate, hear of anything that the accused is alleged to have said; or

e) read any document;

without first conferring with the court clerk and learning:

(i)   whether the information is admissible as evidence; and

(ii) the purpose of its being admitted as evidence.

CHAPTER 12

LICENSING

One of the more important of a magistrate's remaining administrative duties is the control of the sale of intoxicating liquor and of some legal betting within the jurisdictional area of his court.

Means of control

The control is exercised by the issue of licences, applications for which are made in public to a number of magistrates sitting as a "licensing committee", having been elected by the Bench to do so. At the hearing of an application for a licence, other interested parties, such as people who live near to where the intoxicating liquor is to be sold or the betting to take place, police officers, and even business rivals, may attend and voice their objections to the granting of the licence.

Magistrates must, of course, comply with the pertinent Acts of Parliament and have regard to decisions of higher courts on points of law but, otherwise, they should base their licensing decisions on what is best for the public at large.

Unless the licensing committee is advised by its clerk that an Act of Parliament or judicial ruling states otherwise, there is no question, for instance, of an applicant having to prove his application, or an objector his objection, beyond all reasonable doubt. Again, magistrates may listen to and rely on hearsay evidence – although how much reliance they put on that hearsay evidence will obviously depend on the circumstances of the application and the nature of the hearsay evidence.

The honest approach

Magistrates must, however, be honest in their approach to an application. For instance, some magistrates are critical of the existence of betting shops in any circumstances – they would, left to themselves, do away with such shops altogether. Parliament has, however, authorised the general existence of betting shops, although leaving it to magistrates to decide where it is appropriate for them to be. A magistrate may not refuse a betting shop licence solely because he is against them; he must accept that betting shops are legal and proper and decide each application on its own merits, although, of course, the Bench will have regard for their general policy for their own district.

Licensing application procedure

No Act of Parliament or regulation states the procedure to be adopted during a licensing application.

Most courts, however, adopt this procedure:

   a) the applicant's advocate outlines his application;

   b) the applicant and his supporting witnesses are called to the witness box in turn, where (usually, but not necessarily, on oath) they are:

     (i) examined-in-chief by the applicant's advocate; and

     (ii) cross-examined by the objectors in turn;

   c) the objectors, in turn, state their objections from the witness box (usually, but not necessarily, on oath), and are cross-examined by the applicant or his advocate; and

   d) the applicant or his advocate may make a final address to the Bench.

This procedure, although the one generally accepted, may be varied. If it is to be varied, however, it is wise for the chairman or court clerk to announce what procedure will be followed, otherwise people will be bobbing up and down at inconvenient moments and tempers will be frayed.

Licensing law and procedure

There is much licensing law, and some of it is not easily understood. Furthermore, the formalities with which an applicant for a licence must apply must be strictly enforced, although they, too, are not always understood by the applicants. Therefore, the wise magistrate relies on the advice given to him by his clerk, after, of course, having listened carefully to anything an advocate may have had to say.

Further concise information on licensing practice and procedure may be found in the Shaw and Sons publication *"Licensing Applications – A Practioner's Guide"* by Tony Kavanagh and Roger F. March (ISBN 0 7219 1121 8).

CHAPTER 13

THE CLERK

The justices' clerk

Every petty sessions division has a justices' clerk who is responsible for the administration of its court. A justices' clerk is usually a solicitor or barrister. The great majority of clerkships are now full-time appointments. Some divisions are not large enough to have a full-time clerk to themselves, and so share one with another division.

Duties of a justices' clerk

It would not be practicable in this book to list and explain all the duties and responsibilities of a justices' clerk, since, in addition to the work they do in the public's and magistrates' eyes, they have wide administrative responsibilities, of which these are a mere sample:

a) the collection and forwarding to the appropriate authority of fines levied by the court;

b) the receiving and distributing of maintenance payments;

c) the administrative work of the licensing justices;

d) the preparation and distribution of innumerable returns; and

e) the documentary preparation for trials and the documentary work that results from committal proceedings.

A justices' clerk is the most important person in the judicial life of his petty sessional division, since it is he who sets the standard – not only for his staff, but for his magistrates too. He is responsible for arranging the instruction of his newly appointed magistrates and, if he is wise, urges the senior members of his Bench to attend periodic lectures. He is required to keep a list of magistrates' attendances in court and to ensure that they do not sit too infrequently or too often. Further, and particularly in small divisions, he has to iron out

140

the various differences between his magistrates. Over and above all this, he is the guide and adviser to all his magistrates. He alone can make his court happy and efficient; and unless a court is both happy and efficient, the public, whom it serves, will suffer.

The task of a justices' clerk is not an easy one and, therefore, magistrates should not add to his difficulties by making demands of him that are outside the scope of his duties. They certainly should not make approaches to, or have discussions about the workings of the court with, members of his staff behind his back.

A magistrate need not necessarily accept the advice of his justices' clerk, although he is wise always to consider it carefully. But he must remember that a justices' clerk and his magistrate are partners: business partners, whose product is justice.

The court clerk

In the courts of small areas, the justices' clerk himself usually acts as court clerk, but in a larger centre where two or more courts are often in session at the same time, his role is more administrative.

Court clerks (apart, of course, from the justices' clerk himself) need not necessarily have the qualifications of a solicitor or a barrister but they have other professional qualifications which are set down by the Home Office as being necessary requirements. A court clerk has a difficult and troublesome task to perform. Theoretically he has no authority (for instance, strict etiquette demands that an advocate addresses his reply to "your Worships", although it answers a question from the court clerk), yet, in practice, he is required to control the flow of the court's business; arbitrate (through his chairman) on disputes between advocates; when necessary, take notes of the evidence; and guide and advise his chairman.

A magistrate must never abdicate to a court clerk his responsibility for making a decision. A magistrate is encouraged to seek his court clerk's advice on questions of law and procedure during a trial, but he must always remember that his clerk gives "advice" and not "instruction". A court clerk's advice must be most carefully considered, but – and this is important – it must also be balanced with or against anything that either or both advocates may have said on the subject; in the end, the decision is the magistrate's and his alone.

Circumstances when a court clerk may advise the magistrates

During criminal trials

Lord Goddard, when he was Lord Chief Justice, made a number of pronouncements as to the situations in which magistrates may seek their court clerk's advice. The effect of these pronouncements may be summarised thus:

1. The court clerk should not retire with his magistrates as a matter of course. When the magistrates make up their mind on the Bench and without retiring, the court clerk should not join their whispered deliberations as a matter of course.

2. Magistrates may seek their clerk's advice by asking him to retire with them or join their whispered deliberations on the Bench about:

   (i)   questions of law;

   (ii) questions that are of law and fact mixed, although the advice asked for must be on the legal facet of the question only;

   (iii) the court's practice and procedure;

   (iv) if the clerk has taken a note of it, the evidence that has been given (and the magistrates may read the notes);

   (v)   the penalties prescribed by law for the particular offence;

   (vi) the sentences that have been imposed by other magistrates of this and neighbouring petty sessions areas in respect of similar offences to that being tried (this is so that there may be some uniformity of sentences); and

   (vii) matters that follow a conviction, *i.e.* the disqualification from driving of a motorist, or the endorsement of his licence and the situation concerning penalty points.

3. A clerk should go to the magistrates' retiring room or join their whispered deliberation only when specifically asked to do so. Furthermore, having given the required advice, he should immediately return to the court or withdraw from the deliberations, leaving the magistrates to continue their deliberations and arrive at a decision without him.

4. It is proper for a court clerk to point out to the magistrates when there is a question of law of which they appear to be unaware. He must not, however, do more than draw attention to the existence of the question or point of law, unless the magistrates then go on to seek his advice.

5. Magistrates must *not* ask their court clerk:

   (i) which witnesses are telling the truth or about any other question of pure fact;

   (ii) whether the accused is innocent or guilty; or

   (iii) what actual sentence they should impose on a convicted accused.

During a matrimonial dispute

In 1954, the President of what was then the Probate, Divorce and Admiralty Division of the High Court made a pronouncement, a part of which reads:

"Nevertheless, it is at least as important in cases of this class as in other cases dealt with by Magistrates' Courts that the decision should be that of the justices themselves, and not that of the justices and their clerk; and that not only should this be so in fact, but that nothing should be done to give the parties or the public the impression that the clerk is influencing the decision. I am, therefore, in complete agreement with the Lord Chief Justice that it should not be regarded as a matter of course that, if the justices retire to consider their decision, the clerk should retire with them. Moreover, whether the justices invite the clerk to retire with them, or send for him in the course of their deliberations, I agree that the clerk should return to his place in court as soon as the justices release him, leaving them to complete their deliberations alone. Bearing in mind that domestic proceedings are often lengthy and may involve points of law in relation to the complaint itself or the amount of maintenance, and that this court insists that a proper note of the evidence must be kept, and that, in the event of an appeal, justices must be prepared to state the reasons for their decision, I recognise that more often than not magistrates may properly wish to refresh their recollection of the evidence by recourse to the clerk's note, or to seek this advice about the law, before coming to their decision..."

The clerk to the justices may, if asked to do so by the Bench or, if he thinks it necessary, advise a Bench as to the matters within his remit, even if he was not in court during the whole or any part of the trial.

A court clerk's dilemma

A magistrate is not only behaving improperly, but is also being unfair if he asks his court clerk:

a) for a *decision* on any subject whatsoever; or

b) for *advice* on a subject whereon a clerk is not allowed to give advice.

A court clerk – especially if he is not the justices' clerk – cannot easily refuse such a request from his magistrates and yet an adverse comment by an appellant court is always taken as personal criticism, not of the magistrates but of the court clerk. Thus, by asking for improper help from the court clerk, the magistrates may be hazarding his career.

CHAPTER 14

THE ADVOCATES

A trial can proceed in an orderly manner and the Bench have a reasonable chance of arriving at the correct verdict only if the rules of evidence, procedure, and etiquette are obeyed by everyone taking part in the trial. Should one advocate obey those rules, while the other disobeys them, inevitably it is the disobedient advocate who will gain an advantage. A chairman of a Bench must, therefore, ensure that the three sets of rules are obeyed and, in order to do so, must know something of the duties and responsibilities of professional advocates.

An advocate's duty
No matter in what type of case or for which side he is appearing, an advocate has three specific obligations to the Bench that override even those he has to his client.

An advocate must:

a) tell the Bench of *all* the law (Acts of Parliament, regulations, and decided cases) that is pertinent to the issue before the court (disclosing that which is unfavourable to his client as well as that which favours him);

b) not mislead the Bench by pretending either;

   (i) that his witnesses will prove something that he knows they cannot; or

   (ii) that a witness has said something that he has not;

   and

c) base his arguments only on the testimony of those who have given evidence, and not volunteer information to the Bench that has not been given on oath by a witness.

Once an advocate has complied with these three obligations, he may argue that the pertinent law should be interpreted in a manner that is favourable to his client. Equally, so long as he does not distort or wrongly state the testimony of witnesses, he may argue that the testimony must be inaccurate, should not be accepted or should be so viewed as to favour his client.

The obligations of a criminal prosecutor

A prosecutor is there to present the prosecution's case against the accused and to assist the Bench in learning whether that case has properly been proved.

A prosecutor's duty is primarily to the Bench and *not* to the client or organisation whom he represents.

So long as he has presented the case against the accused in the best light and has rigorously tested the accused's defence by questioning the accused and his witnesses, a prosecutor should be disinterested in the final verdict, whether it be guilty or not guilty.

A prosecutor must subject the accused and his witnesses to a searching and analytical (but courteous) cross-examination; he must not mislead or bully them.

Since a prosecutor's task is to reveal the truth of his case against the accused and not to "win at all costs", it is not part of his duty to hide defects in his case or to protect the witnesses whom he has called to testify.

Indeed, an allegation of improper behaviour on the part of a prosecutor's witness – be he a civilian or a police officer – that has a bearing on the issue before the court should be thoroughly examined by the accused's advocate, unhampered by the Bench or prosecutor.

Should it become obvious or seem probable during the course of the trial that the case against the accused cannot be sustained, the prosecutor must not attempt to fabricate a better case.

American Bar ethics

Americans are noted for the clarity with which they state a principle and one of the canons of professional ethics of the American Bar graphically and concisely sets out a prosecutor's duty. The canon states:

"The primary duty of a lawyer engaged in public prosecution

is not to convict, but see that justice is done. The suppression of facts or the secreting of witnesses capable of establishing the innocence of the accused is reprehensible."

Witnesses whom the prosecutor does not intend to call

A prosecutor is obliged to inform the accused or those acting for him of the names and addresses of any witnesses of whom the prosecutor is aware but does not intend to call to give evidence for the prosecution. The information must be given in time for the accused to interview the witnesses and prepare his defence.

An accused is under no similar obligation to assist the prosecutor, nor, for that matter, is a complainant or defendant to a civil dispute under an obligation to give such information to his or her opponent.

Laymen as prosecutors

A wide variety of people including Trading Standards Officers, Health and Safety Inspectors, and local government officials, are allowed to act as prosecutors in the Magistrates' Courts but, in practice, the majority of prosecutions are conducted by prosecuting solicitors or barristers from the Crown Prosecution Service.

One should sympathise with lay prosecutors. Seldom are they trained for the task, which usually requires a mental approach that is the opposite of that needed to ensure success in their chosen calling. Often, both the individual and his superiors regard advocacy as a tiresome chore which, even if undertaken with enthusiasm, will reflect no credit on the individual. Lay prosecutors, in particular, find it difficult to acquire the required objectivity, especially when prosecuting those whom they know to be guilty, yet who may escape conviction because of some rule of evidence: for such prosecutors the temptation to disregard the rule must be great indeed.

Although a Bench may sympathise with lay prosecutors, it must not favour or help them. If those who institute prosecutions entrust them to inadequate or ignorant prosecutors, they must take the consequences and not rely on the magistrates or their court clerks to assist the prosecutor.

The trial rules must be enforced as strictly in the case of an inadequate and inexperienced prosecutor as when the prosecutor is a man of ability.

An accused's advocate and an advocate appearing in a civil case

Subject to his general duty as an advocate to inform the court of *all* the pertinent law and avoid misleading it as to the facts, an accused advocate's duty is primarily to his client.

An accused's advocate must accept his client's version of the events giving rise to the charge. He may, indeed he should, advise that an apparently impossible story is unlikely to be believed, but the decision as to what will be the defence is, and always must be, the accused's.

There is one, and only one, circumstance under which an advocate must not tell or advance his client's story, and that is when the client admits to his advocate that the story is false: if, then, the client insists on telling the untrue story, the advocate must refuse to act for him. Although no longer acting for the client, the advocate must thereafter keep secret the client's intention to lie, not telling anyone – the court, the police, nor, even, any other lawyer whom the client may consult – of that intention.

Should an accused delay telling his advocate that his defence is a lie until after the trial has started, the advocate may not then abandon the accused, but must continue to appear for him. The advocate must not, however, by calling his client or by the phraseology of his questions, advance the untrue defence: he must, on the other hand:

a) test the memory and truthfulness of the prosecutor's witnesses by questioning them; and

b) ensure that the prosecutor obeys the rules of evidence and procedure.

Technicalities

Unless the offence with which the accused is charged is one of the very few exceptions, the burden of proving the accused's guilt is on the prosecutor. Thus, an accused's advocate must take advantage of every technicality available to him as well as of inadequacies on the part of the prosecutor, and the magistrates should not hold it against him or his client that he has done so. An accused's advocate must quickly and fearlessly, albeit courteously, protect his client from improper questions or departures from the rules of evidence.

An advocate in a civil trial has the same duties and obligations as the accused's advocate.

Advocacy

A magistrate's task is made easier when the prosecutor and the accused's advocate are knowledgeable, experienced and courteous advocates. However, magistrates often have to suffer advocates who are long-winded, pompous, and ignorant of the rules; and then the Bench must ensure that neither side gains an advantage by disobeying the rules whether deliberately or through ignorance.

Finally, no matter how indignant at or impatient with the accused's advocate the magistrates may be, they must not vent their wrath on the accused.

CHAPTER 15

THE UNREPRESENTED

Now that the scope of legal aid and the provisions of various Criminal Justice Acts have been extended to domestic proceedings and criminal proceedings respectively, the number of unrepresented accused, complainants and defendants appearing before the magistrates is decreasing. It will further decrease as the magistrates – to whom application for legal aid is made in respect of criminal, but not civil, trials – appreciate that it is not only fair to the individual, but helpful to themselves that legal aid should be granted.

There are still, nevertheless, a large number of unfortunates who have to plead their causes unaided.

Causes of tension

Not only does an advocate prepare his client's case and present it at the trial, but he also acts as a guide and friend, giving his client confidence to cope with what is usually an ordeal.

Without an advocate, an accused person or a party to civil dispute is bewildered by the hustle and bustle and apparent indifference of those who throng the court; and when to this is added his apprehension that the Bench's verdict will affect his future life, it is not surprising that he is on edge and in need of tactful and patient handling if he is to leave the court believing that he has been fairly dealt with.

Witnesses and legal aid

People who have been arrested or summoned to court are often ignorant of court procedure and may arrive unprepared for the trial. Such a person should, therefore, always be asked by the court clerk before the trial starts whether he is ready to meet the charges and whether those witnesses on whom he intends to rely are in court. If it then appears that he is not ready for the trial, it should be postponed.

Those who have no advocates should be told of their right to ask the magistrates or the Legal Aid Board (as the case may be) for legal aid and given a chance to make their application.

The preliminaries

Whether the accused is represented or not, it is always necessary for a Bench to ensure that anyone appearing before them understands the charge or allegation against him and, if he admits it, that he realises the implications of doing so. When such a person is not represented, magistrates must take even greater pains in this respect.

When someone who has no advocate denies the charge, he is not necessarily required to conduct his case standing in the dock, but may be invited to sit at a desk or table and provided with writing material. This practice varies from court to court. There is no reason why a trained advocate should be given physical advantages over his untrained opponent. The opponent must not be given the impression that he is at a disadvantage solely because he has not employed an advocate.

Before the trial starts, the court clerk should carefully and clearly explain the procedure of the trial, so that a man without an advocate knows what is to come.

The trained opponent

Even when his opponent is unrepresented, a professional advocate must test his opponent's case with searching, skilful questions. Magistrates must ensure hat no advocate takes advantage of an unrepresented opponent's lack of expert knowledge and isolated state as there are advocates who would do just this.

The court's attitude

Magistrates must, of course, be tolerant of the delays caused by the layman's inexperience and ignorance, and overlook angry or indignant outbursts that may be the result of his frustrating realisation that opposing witnesses do not necessarily tell the truth. No matter how sympathetic for the layman's immediate predicament magistrates may be, however, they must be no less impartial than when both sides are represented by advocates. Magistrates must make allowance for the fact that the unrepresented accused will, probably, not put his case in the best light, but if, having made that allowance, they are satisfied beyond all reasonable doubt of his guilt, they must convict him.

As young and inexperienced advocates know all too well, it is difficult to phrase a series of questions without lapsing into narration, and if curtly told to confine himself to questions, a layman's examination of a witness soon deteriorates into a "You did", "I didn't" exchange.

When there is a danger of this happening, the court clerk must go to the layman's aid by having the layman narrate his version of the various parts of the episode, and then transposing the narration into a series of questions to the witnesses.

Inevitably, the trial of an unrepresented layman takes much time, and makes the tasks of the magistrates, their clerk and the trained opponent the more difficult, and it is for that reason that the true worth of the Bench, the clerk and the advocate is never more discernible than when they are coping with an unrepresented accused.

CHAPTER 16

THE MAGISTRATE OUT OF COURT

SOCIAL OBLIGATIONS

In addition to his judicial duties undertaken in court, a magistrate is expected to perform other tasks at his home and elsewhere. These tasks are sometimes time-consuming and irritating, particularly if the magistrate is a member of a small community, but nevertheless they must be undertaken with care and dignity.

A magistrate, together with ministers of religion, senior police officers, doctors, and lawyers, is considered sufficiently responsible to witness the signing of various important documents and, in addition, is empowered on some occasions to take Statutory Declarations and administer oaths.

Although a magistrate is under no obligation to advise on, or ensure the truth of, the contents of the document concerned, when he is undertaking one of these tasks it is advisable for him to read the document and, particularly, any instructional notes that are attached to it, so that he may learn:

a) whether a magistrate is empowered to perform the required task (and he should assume he is not empowered unless the document or its note specifically states that he is); and

b) whether he is required to:

    (i)   witness a signature;

    (ii)   take a Statutory Declaration;

    (iii) administer an oath; or

    (iv) himself volunteer or confirm information.

Patently, a magistrate should refuse to accept a document unless it is typed or written in ink, and should not perform any of these duties for his spouse; indeed, he is wise not to do so for a close relative.

Witnessing a signature

The signing of certain documents is required to be done in the presence of a responsible person in order to diminish the chance of an undetected fraud being perpetrated, and therefore, no mater how well he may know the signatory and his signature, or apparently unimportant the document may be, a magistrate should insist on the document being signed in his presence. Should the document already have been signed, it is *not* sufficient for the signatory to acknowledge or declare that the signature is his or over-write it with a dry pen: a fresh signature must be written in the magistrate's presence.

Although many signatories will be impatient with, and indignant at, this insistence on formality, it is essential. Furthermore, the office of magistrate is important enough for its holder to demand formality.

A magistrate needs to:

a) ensure that he is entitled to witness the signature;

b) watch the signature being written;

c) date the document the day on which it was signed; and

d) himself sign the document in the appropriate place, adding his title of Justice of the Peace.

Consent to an Adoption Order

Normally, that is all the magistrate is required to do. If, however, the document is a Consent to an Adoption Order, he is required also to inform the signatory of its effect which, briefly, is that the signatory is signing away all his or her rights as a parent to those who are adopting the child (once an Adoption Order has been made it cannot be revoked); unless, of course, he or she changes his or her mind before the order is actually made, in which case the court should be informed at once.

The signatory must produce to the magistrate the child's birth certificate as well as the form of consent unless the certificate has been identified by the other parent. In practice, however, in order to ensure that the application is not rendered defective, the magistrate is wise to have the certificate produced to him in all cases. When it is produced, the magistrate is required to sign the consent.

A form of consent to a child's adoption, signed by a mother, may not be produced as evidence of her consent unless the child is six weeks old when the document is signed. However, it should be emphasised that these matters should preferably be dealt with through the justices' clerk or by a member of the Family Proceedings panel if time is short.

Taking a Statutory Declaration and administering an oath

The making of a Statutory Declaration or the taking of an oath at the magistrate's home or elsewhere is as serious a step as the taking of an oath as a witness in a law court's witness box. Should the document whose truth is being sworn to or declared contain a deliberate falsehood, the deponent may be charged with perjury, and in that event the magistrate will be required to testify at the deponent's trial as to the manner in which he administered the declaration or oath. It is, therefore, important for a magistrate to conduct himself with a dignity that will impress on the deponent the seriousness of the declaration or oath.

The magistrate should:

a) carefully read the document and any instructional notes in order to learn whether;

  (i) a magistrate is empowered to perform the required task; and

  (ii) it is a Statutory Declaration or an oath that is required;

b) watch the deponent sign in the proper place;

c) take the declaration or administer the oath;

d) initial any deletions, alterations, and interlineations in the document;

e) date the declaration or oath; and

f) sign it in the proper place, adding his title of Justice of the Peace.

When taking a Statutory Declaration or administering an oath, the magistrate and the deponent should be standing, and the jurat (as the declaration and oath are referred to by lawyers) should be spoken, sentence by sentence, by the magistrate and repeated by the deponent.

The making of a Statutory Declaration and the taking of an oath is a solemn and important undertaking and should be treated as such.

Statutory Declaration

No bible is required for a Statutory Declaration, the wording of which is:

"I, John Smith, do solemnly and sincerely declare that this (indicating his signature) is my name and handwriting, and I make this declaration conscientiously believing the same to be true and by virtue of the Statutory Declarations Act 1835."

An oath

To take an oath, a Christian is required to hold in his uplifted right hand a copy of the New Testament (a Roman Catholic may require it to be a Douai version), and a Jew, whose head must be covered while he takes the oath, a copy of the Old Testament. Followers of other religions will consider themselves bound by the oath only if they are sworn on their own sacred book (Moslems, for instance, require a copy of the Koran), while the forms of oath recognised by some religions are complicated both in wording and performance. Should the particular sacred book not be available or the form of oath not be known, the deponent may affirm (*see below*).

In those areas where there is a large non-Christian and non-Jewish community, a magistrate might consider it worthwhile asking his clerk to provide him with instructions as to how to swear the members of that community. When, however, a magistrate is doubtful as to the form the oath should take, he would be foolish to do other than delay the ceremony until he has taken his clerk's advice.

The jurat, or wording of the oath, for a Christian and a Jew is:

"I, John Smith, swear by Almighty God that this (indicating his signature) is my name and handwriting and the contents of this document are true."

An affirmation

Instead of swearing on oath, a deponent may affirm that the contents of the document are true.

In such an event, the magistrate should carefully read the document and alter any references in it from "swearing" to "solemnly and sincerely affirming".

The wording of an affirmation is:

"I, John Smith, do solemnly and sincerely affirm that this (indicating his signature) is my name and handwriting and the contents of this document are true."

Deponents with visual handicaps or persons without speech or where there are language difficulties

When witnessing the signature of a blind or illiterate deponent or taking a deposition from such a person, a magistrate is under an obligation to ensure that the deponent is aware of the contents of the document and its effect, and the purpose of his signing, declaring or swearing to it. Obviously, the magistrate must carefully read the whole of the document to the deponent, and not accept the assurance of the deponent's spouse or friend that the deponent understands it. Should the magistrate himself not understand the contents of the document, or be doubtful, he should refuse to act.

A blind or illiterate person may make a mark if he is unable to write his signature.

Before signing the document himself, the magistrate should write above his signature:

"I having first truly, distinctly, and audibly read over the contents of this document to the said dependent, he being blind (or illiterate), he appeared to understand the same perfectly and made his mark (or signature) thereto in my presence."

When the deponent is deaf, dumb, or cannot speak English, an interpreter must be present, and the magistrate needs to satisfy himself that the interpreter is capable of interpreting accurately.

The interpreter must, at the outset, take the following oath, administered by the magistrate:

"I swear by Almighty God that I will well and truly interpret and translate the contents of this [document] and also the oath to be administered to the deponent and explain to him all such matters and things as shall be required of me to the best of my skill and understanding."

Then, through the interpreter, the magistrate should ensure that the deponent understands the contents of the document and the purport of his signing it or declaring or swearing as to the truth of its contents.

Obviously, it is better that the interpreter should not be the spouse or close relative of the deponent.

In the place where he makes his signature, the magistrate should write:

"Sworn at
in the county of   this   day of   19
through the interpretation of [the interpreter's names] of [the interpreter's address] the said [the interpreter's names] having been first sworn that he would truly and faithfully interpret the contents of this [document] to the deponent [the deponent's names] and that he would truly and faithfully interpret the oath about to be administered unto [the deponent's names]."

Dating and initialling the document

Whether he is witnessing a signature, taking a Statutory Declaration, or administering an oath, the magistrate must insert the date on which the ceremony occurred. Occasionally he will be asked to either ante- or post-date the document, but should refuse to comply with any such improper request: often a document is legally effective only if it is completed on or before a certain date, and by ante- or post-dating it, a magistrate may unwittingly be assisting in a fraud or an abuse of court procedure.

When he has taken a Statutory Declaration or administered an oath, a magistrate is required to read the document again and put his initials in the margin against any insertions, deletions, or alterations, whether made in type or ink, that there may be in order to make obvious any alterations in the document made subsequent to the attendance on him.

If a deponent finds it necessary subsequently to alter the document, he is, in effect, re-writing it and must attend on either the previous or a fresh magistrate to go through the ceremony of signing the document or declaring or swearing as to the truth of its contents as though the first ceremony had not taken place. The magistrate must, for instance, initial all alterations, insertions and deletions, whether they are fresh or were present on the earlier occasion. The magistrate then writes in the words "re-witnessed (re-declared or re-sworn)", signs his name again, and inserts the date on which the second ceremony occurred, which is the effective date of the document.

The signature

There is no laid down style of signature: both the magistrate and the deponent should write their usual signatures.

In case the magistrate is later required to give information as to the deposing, it is useful if he writes his home address after his signature, and (if that is illegible) prints his name below his signature.

Although some courts retain facsimiles of justices' signatures on rubber stamps, magistrates are advised not to have a facsimile at home because, apart from the legality of its use being questionable, it may be stolen and misused by a third party.

The giving or confirming of information by a magistrate

There are occasions when a magistrate is empowered to give or confirm information about a third party, and thereby enable that third party to acquire a privilege that, without the information, would not be available to him. The most frequently occurring example, but by no means the only one, is the acquisition of a passport, for which purpose an applicant is required to supply information and have much of it confirmed by a member of a responsible profession or calling.

No matter how persuasive or plaintive the applicant may be, the magistrate must not confirm or declare any information about him that is not within the magistrate's own personal knowledge.

A magistrate must understand that his office will not protect him from criticism and perhaps even prosecution if those in authority learn that he has assisted in the improper acquisition of a passport or any other privilege or advantage, by lying or telling a half-truth.

A friend of long standing may ask a magistrate, "Please sign this form saying that this information about my daughter is true." Unless he has known, and not merely known of the existence of, the friend's daughter and knows all the information he is being asked to confirm is true, a magistrate must refuse to comply with the request, even though he may court unpopularity, and cause hardship to the daughter.

An application for a passport is but one example of the many reasons why a magistrate may be asked to give or confirm information, and before he complies with such a request he should quietly ask himself, "Do I, honestly, know of my own knowledge, and not merely because someone has told me, that these facts are true?" Unless he can answer with an emphatic "Yes" in respect of *each* fact, the magistrate should decline to sign the document.

The giving of advice

Although magistrates have no legal training apart from their attendances at lectures and courses, laymen often regard them as being experts in all branches of the law, and seek their advice at home, in clubs, and even public houses, on matters that range from wayward offspring, matrimonial disputes, motoring offences, pension rights, the drafting of wills, and hire purchase troubles, to the buying of a house.

Knowing that as a result of his ignorance of the law he may mislead the questioner, and that were he to draft certain documents he might be prosecuted under the Solicitors' Acts, the wise magistrate emphatically refuses to offer advice. Instead, he tells his questioner to consult a solicitor, or seek assistance from a Citizens Advice Bureau, probation officer, or the police.

Magistrates are advised to have the addresses and telephone numbers of these organisations readily available.

Even if he has refused to give advice, a magistrate should never adjudicate on any trial that arises from the events that caused the need for advice, otherwise he may unwittingly gain the reputation of being open to behind-the-scenes persuasion.

When the problem is a legal or vaguely legal one, it is best that the questioner should consult a solicitor, since any of the above-mentioned organisations will, ultimately, have to send him to a solicitor, and the delay may be crucial.

At one time, the cost of legal advice precluded many from seeking it. Today, however, the statutory Legal Aid and Advice scheme, which was instituted under the Legal Aid and Advice Act 1949, brings legal advice within the financial range of the poorest of us.

A magistrate should not advise a questioner to consult a particular solicitor, otherwise it may be thought that, for some improper reason, he favours that solicitor; rather he should give the questioner a list of the solicitors in the district, although he may indicate those who, for instance, regularly practice in the Magistrates' Court. If the magistrate is doubtful which solicitors to suggest, he would be wise to tell the questioner to visit the secretary of the local Law Society or Legal Aid Board.

The acceptance of fees

No matter how much of this time he may give or trouble he may take over these extra-judicial duties, a magistrate must not charge a fee for performing them. Indeed, he ought to refuse any gift for doing this or any other such work, because it is surprising how quick are the unscrupulous to allege that they have, with advantage to themselves, granted a favour to, or even bribed, a person in authority.

JUDICIAL DUTIES

The taking of a statement from a witness who is dangerously ill and unlikely to recover

Occasionally, a magistrate is asked to attend at a hospital, police station, private house, or elsewhere, to take a deposition from a witness who is dangerously ill and is not expected to live long enough to attend court and testify in the normal way. The request may be made by the prosecution (usually the police) or the accused (usually through his solicitor) even if he has not yet been charged and is, therefore, merely a potential accused.

The circumstances under which such a deposition is accepted as evidence and the procedure that must be followed when such a deposition is being recorded are complicated and, therefore, a magistrate should make every effort to have his clerk's assistance while taking the deposition. No matter whether it is the prosecution or the accused who wants the deposition to be taken, the local police will, no doubt, do all they can to locate the justices' clerk or his assistant.

Issuing processes

Most petty sessional divisions have a specified time at which applications may be made to a magistrate to issue a summons or warrant, which is usually before or after the court's business is done. Occasionally, there is a reason why a process should be issued at short notice, for example when the police urgently wish to search a suspect's house and, in that event, an approach may be made to a magistrate when he is away from his court and at an inconvenient hour.

The issuing of summonses and warrants may appear to be a mere routine step, but it is not one that should be undertaken lightly. A magistrate may be personally liable in damages if he issues a process without having the jurisdiction to do so. The wise magistrate therefore insists, when there is time, on his clerk being told of the request and approving of the process before the magistrate signs anything. If the clerk, for any reason, is not available, the magistrate should inquire of the applicant, going to the length of putting him on oath, as to the events that have led up to the request and the reason for it.

A witness summons

Magistrates are often asked by both prosecutors and defendants to issue summonses ordering witnesses to attend court. A magistrate has the power to order a witness to attend only a committal or a civil or criminal summary trial that will take place in the county for which he is a magistrate: a magistrate has no authority to order a witness to attend at any other than a Magistrates' Court.

When a magistrate is approached to issue a witness summons, he should be satisfied that:

a) proceedings have already been commenced, and a date for trial fixed; and

b) the witness:

  (i) is in England or Wales;

  (ii) is likely to be able to give material evidence or likely to be able to produce a document or thing that will be material evidence; and

  (iii) will not voluntarily attend or produce the document or thing,

before he issues the summons.

Although a magistrate must carefully inquire into the matters listed above, he will normally not refuse to issue the summons, particularly if the request is made by a responsible person.

If a magistrate is satisfied by evidence given on oath not only of the matters listed above, but also that the witness will ignore the summons, he may issue a warrant to arrest the witness and have him brought to the trial. The arrest of a person who is not the defendant is, however, a gross interference with the liberty of the subject and so a magistrate should be most reluctant to issue a warrant, except in the most exceptional circumstances.

Warrants of detention

A magistrate may also be asked to hear an application by or on behalf of the police for an extension of the time permitted to detain a suspect in custody, while they continue their investigations. Such an application will be made after the arrest and before any charge is preferred. Hearings can take place outside normal working hours but must be heard in a courtroom.

CHAPTER 17

THE PITFALLS

A person apart

An appointment to the judicial Bench, whether in a professional or amateur capacity, puts a person apart from his peers and makes him the target of the blandishments and flattery of the unscrupulous. If a magistrate wants to retain his reputation for impartiality and incorruptibility, he must remember that it will be made or marred as much out of court as when actually on the Bench.

Magistrates and the police

The police are represented in a Magistrates' Court more often than any other body of people, and their prosecuting officer – usually a solicitor – is in the court more frequently than any other advocate. The prosecutor is an employee of the Crown Prosecution Service and, for that reason, privileges and favours offered by a police officer should be refused, and a magistrate should be reluctant to accept either official or unofficial, individual or collective invitations to entertainment and hospitality from the police. Certainly a magistrate should never privately and informally discuss with a police officer or Crown Prosecution solicitor anything connected, however remotely, with his office.

Magistrates are advised to dissuade the police from making public references to "Your Worships' police" and the police's willingness to assist the Bench. Any indication that the magistracy is connected with, has obligations to, or administrative authority over the police, or any other prosecuting body or official, dangerously undermines the public's belief in the independence and impartiality of the Bench – a belief that is of a recent origin and could easily be shattered.

The detached magistrate

A magistrate must never allow expediency, personal interest or embarrassment to persuade him into doing something against the dictates of his conscience. Unless he is confident that his approach to a particular trial will be detached and that he is unafraid of the consequences to himself, he should refuse to adjudicate at that particular trial. He need not publicly announce his reasons for refusing to adjudicate.

A public trust

A magistrate needs to try each case with down-to-earth common sense, yet his attitude to his judicial role and magisterial office must be idealistic. The public have put their trust in the lay magistracy. They look to each of their magistrates as individuals to shield them from abuses of the power of the State, to protect them from wrongful conviction, and to punish those who are proved wrongdoers.

To be so trusted is to be honoured: to accept the honour is to undertake an onerous obligation to the public at large.

INDEX

A

B

C

D

E

F

G

H

I

J